UNTAPPED TALENT

Aron Mercer

UNTAPPED TALENT

A Practical Guide for Hiring and Retaining Neurodivergent Staff

The Disability Studies Collection

Collection Editors

Damian Mellifont

& Jennifer Smith-Merry

LPP

I dedicate this book to neurodivergent people, working hard wherever they are, employers bending the rules to let them thrive and my beautiful family, Louise, Lachie and Harvey, for tolerating my early morning starts and absent weekends.

First published in 2024 by Lived Places Publishing

British Library Cataloguing in Publication Data
A CIP record for this book is available from the British Library

ISBN: 9781916704251 (pbk)
ISBN: 9781916704275 (ePDF)
ISBN: 9781916704268 (ePUB)

Cover design by Fiachra McCarthy
Book design by Rachel Trolove of Twin Trail Design
Typeset by Newgen Publishing UK

Lived Places Publishing
Long Island
New York 11789

www.livedplacespublishing.com

Abstract

Untapped Talent explores the unique challenges and untapped potential of neurodivergent people in the workplace. Through a combination of lived experience, storytelling, and research, this book provides people leaders and coworkers with a practical guide on inclusive recruitment, retention, and advancement of neurodivergent people. The principles offered can be applied broadly, benefiting many. By addressing biases and stereotypes and breaking down barriers, *Untapped Talent* aims to foster inclusion and belonging and provide actionable steps for today's workplaces.

Keywords

1. Diversity and inclusion
2. Workplace diversity
3. Inclusion
4. Autism
5. ADHD
6. Recruitment
7. Employee retention
8. Neurodiversity
9. Disability employment
10. Neuroinclusion

Contents

Author's note

This book is not intended to be a clinical or academic examination of neurodivergence, but rather a practical guide based on lived and professional experience. Whenever I use a lived experience scenario to illustrate a topic, I have changed the name of the individual and their employer to protect their confidentiality. I appreciate some irony in changing each subject's name in the context of supporting disclosure in an inclusive workplace, while acknowledging that it is often poor workplace culture that leads neurodivergent people to hide. Finally, the preferred gendered pronouns, she/her, he/him and they/them are used for each lived experience scenario based on the subject's preference or my interpretation.

Content warning

This book discusses topics that may be sensitive or triggering for some readers, including discussions of mental health challenges, discrimination, and stressful workplace experiences. Reader discretion is advised.

Learning objectives

Untapped Talent is designed to help readers to:

1. **Recognise bias and stereotypes:** Identify and challenge common biases and stereotypes about neurodivergent people in the workplace.

2. **Understand employment challenges and strengths:** Improve understanding of the unique employment challenges experienced by neurodivergent individuals and untapped strengths they can offer in the workplace.

3. **Develop inclusive practices:** Learn practical strategies and best practices for creating a neuroinclusive work environment.

4. **Enhance recruitment processes:** Gain insights and practical strategies into how to adapt recruitment processes to be more accessible and inclusive for neurodivergent candidates.

5. **Support neurodivergent employees:** Understand the importance of providing ongoing support and accommodations for neurodivergent employees to ensure their success and well-being.

Foreword

Kurt Schoeffer, Group CEO auticon

I first encountered Aron in 2017, shortly after he helped launch a social enterprise in Australia that employed autistic people to provide technology services. I was struck then, as I am now, by Aron's energy, curiosity, and passion. It was a surprise, but a welcome one, when Aron asked me to write a foreword for *Untapped Talent*.

It may seem strange that someone with a deep background in corporate finance, based in Germany, would take an interest in a small service business on the other side of the world. Prior to my involvement in auticon it would have been. I have spent my whole career in the IT industry and very often was with the right people at the right place at the right time. When I was approached by the first impact fund in Germany, I immediately fell in love with the concept of a social impact investment. Using business methodology to help solve social problems just makes so much sense to me. When the investors asked me if I would help them to get auticon started, I did not hesitate to say, of course I will help you, for 3 or 6 months, and now I am still here after 12 years running this amazing business.

Our success and growth over the last 15 years are testament to the power of diversity. We are determined to continue to lead by example and set new benchmarks for workplace diversity and inclusion. Our team of people with wide-ranging skills and professional backgrounds are all challenging outdated assumptions on who can and cannot contribute to a workplace. The varied social and cultural settings that auticon operates in today has further served to lend us a richer understanding of diversity and inclusion. We will continue to share this understanding with the world.

Organisations are waking up to the importance of neuroinclusion, as they recognise this affects a significant number of their current staff and likely even more of their future employees. It will be vital for organisations to have the expertise, lived experience, and capacity to transform into better working environments where all can thrive. Companies who have an answer on the challenges of a fast-changing world will not only be ahead in the fight for talent but also achieve much better business results.

As Neurodivergent brains operate differently to the majority of the population, they may provide a different perspective to business and client problems. Neurodivergent and neurotypical people can work together and complement each other's strengths. This can unlock greater value for companies and foster greater innovation through diversity of thought.

I share Aron's insight that managers lack practical knowledge about neurodiversity and are fearful of doing or saying the wrong thing. This is why more work needs to be done to educate, train, and support managers in roles.

Building up our autistic majority business was a lot of work, but not rocket science. Every company on this globe which is

willing to appreciate diversity and is prepared to throw traditional recruitment criteria overboard can do the same. Each of
the readers of this book can become an ambassador for neurodiversity and grow into exciting roles by being a neuro-confident
leader.

Introduction

The room was a little small for the gathering. Early November on a Tuesday afternoon, public servants shuffled in to hear about a topic few understood, neurodiversity. Some had a personal interest, an autistic daughter, a dyslexic friend, or an undisclosed diagnosis they kept as a closely guarded secret. Others carried the diversity and inclusion flag and were the first to commit to any such meeting. Still, to be honest, most were there because a manager or department head had asked them to attend the meeting.

This was to be the last meeting for the day before the office adjourned for the Melbourne Cup horse race, Australia's equivalent of the Kentucky Derby. The famous Race 8 started at 3.20 p.m. so my team and I were on the clock to wrap our presentation in a timely manner. There was a predictable mixture of polite curiosity, enthusiastic hope, discussions of practical accommodations, and questions about the recruitment process. Some were surprised that a company dedicated to providing meaningful careers for neurodivergent people would focus training efforts on employed and "normal" managers and staff.

The meeting finished and I was invited to a much larger room where a projector was showing the race that stops the nation, as the Melbourne Cup is affectionally known. It was only now that the real questions surfaced. Over soft drinks and triangle sandwiches, the fears, doubts, and biases of managers bubbled out, slowly at first then in a rush. "How do we make sure the environment is perfect?" "What about team fit?", "How do we know if they can do the job?", "Can autistic people even talk?" "Aren't we all 'on the spectrum' a little bit?"

Untapped Talent will address the questions from the second informal gathering, those that managers dare not ask in a public forum like the upstairs' meeting. Questions born from fears of difference, ignorance, and political correctness. My aim is to provide people leaders and coworkers with a practical guide on inclusive recruitment, retainment, and advancement of neurodivergent people. The principles covered can be applied to anyone, and, as is often the case, where a change is made for some, it can also benefit many. In writing this book my hope is barriers are broken down and muffled questions answered so that greater inclusivity can be realised.

Untapped Talent will draw on my lived experience as a neurodivergent individual, as well as professional experience in business development, technology, and social enterprise. I consider myself fortunate to have met Mike Tozer, a British social entrepreneur, who in 2017 was on the cusp of launching a technology service business that employed autistic people. From the early days of launching Xceptional in Australia to my work now supporting neuroinclusion through advocacy and education, my goal is to challenge stereotypes and bias, while providing practical steps for employers.

About me

Growing up I was a paradox – I loved creative writing, and I told stories constantly – but I could not spell and was in the "special class", until diagnosed with Attention Deficit Hyperactivity Disorder (ADHD) at 12 years of age.

I never pursued my love of storytelling as the tools of spelling, grammar, and planning eluded me. Verbally, I can happily roll off detailed stories, but the constraints of writing curtailed my ability to fully express my thoughts. The prospect of ever writing a book seemed entirely unfathomable. Now, with the help of technology, I am able to do so. Tools like automatic spellcheck, shared docs for collaboration, focus time on my phone to limit the use of distracting news and social media apps, AI, and voice to text make a daunting task like writing a book possible.

In a professional setting I have spoken with thousands of neurodivergent people who are constrained in some way. Some have social anxiety or sensory sensitivities, which make meeting new people in situations like job interviews overwhelming, confusing, and distressing. They may struggle with ambiguous language or lack of clear instructions. Many tell me that they do not understand what's asked of them in a job interview and spend a lot of time second guessing themselves. Some have acute sensitivity to stimuli like noise or bright lights. Most report to having to "mask", which is a common term referring to acting in certain ways to fit in and appear like everybody else. Collectively, these factors add up to constraints, which can hold neurodivergent people back.

On the other side of the equation, I have listened to hiring managers who would like to try alternative approaches to recruitment but are constrained by policy and process. They may work for a government department or large corporation that has a strict framework around merit-based recruitment and advancement. Often these frameworks are outdated, as are the employer's job descriptions, which at best loosely fit the roles being advertised. Others need to rely on panel interviews and consensus when making hiring decisions. Research has shown that hiring decisions are heavily influenced by biases. These biases, such as affinity bias and familiarity bias (which we will talk about later), act as invisible shields, unconscious barriers which determine who progresses, and who doesn't.

If policy, process, and bias weren't enough, the constraints of cost and time layer pressure on hiring managers to decide and move on. Having been a hiring manager under such pressure I can understand the tendency to hire obvious candidates rather than those who present a little differently. The hiring managers I speak with are all stretched and near capacity. Often their approval for headcount has been a long time coming and their workload and that of their team is already under pressure. Therefore, asking them to consider something different requires additional effort, and I recognise that comes at a cost.

Through storytelling, and practical application, I aim to break down employment barriers by sharing lived experiences that connect social identity and place. My hope is these stories and suggestions are both enjoyable to read and relevant for the hiring manager who needs practical advice to pursue a different approach to recruitment and management.

1
What on earth is neurodiversity?

The radio studio waiting room was a time capsule-filled with items you might find in an upmarket garage sale. Vintage radios and microphones stood alongside posters of appreciation from a children's hospital fundraiser and a breakfast show star of the 1990s. Budget tea, coffee, and mismatched cups reminded me that this was not a commercial station. The one current fixture is a large digital clock displaying the time. The clock is wasted on me as I check my phone 200 times a day and am generally an excellent judge of time. I check the big clock anyway – you can never be too sure!

I'm preparing for a live radio interview. Neurodiversity has become newsworthy. In the lead up to my presence in the waiting room the producer has been a little casual for my liking. I've asked for some guidance on questions and been given broad "areas" to discuss. Rather than persisting in my queries, I relax as best as I can by distracting myself with the displays. I enter the studio and the conversation starts. Radio presenters mention the time a lot, perhaps to stop drivers checking their phones. They also continually say their name; I wonder if I should do the same?

After all, it's not my show and I will likely be forgotten after the three o'clock news. I resist the urge. The presenter reminds the listeners of my name, the topic we are discussing, and, of course, the time. We cover topics such as employment barriers, skills shortages, and school leavers. Midway through the conversation it dawns on me, neurodiversity has a branding problem.

While information availability about neurodiversity is increasing, knowledge about neurodivergence in the workplace remains lacking. Aside from neurodivergent individuals and their families, few outside the diversity, equity, and inclusion space really know what neurodiversity means. The listeners to this radio show and the employers I speak with each day have a very limited understanding of it. So, I confess on live radio that, despite knowing I had an ADHD diagnosis, I had no idea what neurodiversity meant until a few years ago. This surprised the presenter, and even the overly casual producer widened their eyes. But it's the truth!

I suspect that I was in the majority for many years in not knowing what neurodiversity means. Other faces of diversity, such as race, age, gender, cultural background, or sexual orientation, have had decades to establish themselves. Neurodiversity is the new kid on the block, the hardest to spot, and the least well understood. For this reason, Untapped Talent will start by covering the basics, from definitions, representations in the media, types of neurominorities such as autism and dyslexia, as well as hacks for inclusion. Throughout this book, I have included stories from the front line. From neurodivergent people, human resource professionals to hiring managers.

Neurodiversity, what you need to know

In the realm of diversity, equity, and inclusion, most attention is focused on elements that you can see. What is talked about and what makes its way into the annual report in relation to diversity is typically visible – think gender, race, physical disabilities, and age as examples. One of the purposes of writing this book is to shine a light on an element of diversity that is often hiding in plain sight. We will cover the language of neurodiversity in detail later, in Chapter 2. For now, I have provided some basic definitions.

Neurodiversity describes the idea that people experience and interact with the world in many different ways; there is no one "right" way of thinking, learning, and behaving (Zindell, 2024). The term "neurodivergent" encompasses a wide range of conditions that involve variations in cognitive functioning, learning styles, and behaviour. Common neurodivergent conditions include autism, ADHD, and dyslexia. It is estimated that between 15 to 20 per cent of the global population are neurodivergent (Doyle, 2020). That is a significant minority, over 1 billion people globally – although, as we will see, both prevenance and disclosure vary among populations, cultures, and gender groups.

For many of us neurodiversity is like emerging technology. You may have heard of it, and even been brave enough to use it in a sentence, but you have not fully understood the new buzzword or worked out yet what it means for you. Think generative AI, internet of things, and the metaverse. Likewise, neurodiversity and its countless misnamed cousins live in many settings, are spoken about by some and understood by few. Below I have outlined common neurominorities, such as autism, ADHD, and dyslexia. I felt it was important to include names for each neurotype, as well as strengths and challenges. Throughout this book, you will hear from the most important voice in the discussion, neurodivergent people themselves. Additionally, neuroinclusive leaders from around the world share their experiences and advice.

Neurodiversity is not a new concept; it dates to the time of Blockbuster, Michael Jordan, and personal computers. The term "neurodiversity" was first coined by Judy Singer in 1998. Singer is an Australian social scientist who first challenged the medical understanding of conditions such as autism being a disability that required treatment (Praslova, 2024). Singer proposed a paradigm shift towards recognising and valuing the diversity of human neurology, arguing that neurological differences are natural variations within the human population, rather than pathological conditions that need to managed or cured. According to Singer, neurodiversity should be embraced as a form of human biodiversity, akin to other types of diversity, such as cultural or genetic diversity. She highlighted the strengths and unique perspectives that neurodivergent individuals bring to society, promoting the idea that their differences can be valuable assets.

While Singer introduced the concept, American journalist Harvey Blume popularised it in his hilarious article "Neurodiversity: On the Neurological Underpinnings of Geekdom" (Blume, 1998). Blume cites John Katz's satirical columns, which challenge the notion that conditions such as autism are deviations from the normal neurotypical brain and are therefore less. Blume suggests that "Neurodiversity may be every bit as crucial for the human race as biodiversity is for life in general. Who can say what form of wiring will prove best at any given moment?" (Smith and Kirby, 2021, p. 5).

In popular culture

Despite the branding problem of neurodiversity, public awareness of conditions like autism, ADHD, and dyslexia is on the rise. A mix of celebrity endorsements, social media reels, news stories, and streaming content have contributed to this awareness. It seems like you can't win a BAFTA award, trend on TikTok, or have a podcast these days without announcing to the world that you are in some way neurodivergent. Representation in media is certainly on the rise. Streaming services like Netflix and Amazon Prime produce shows based on unfathomable amounts of data. So, when you see shows pop up like *Atypical* and *Love on the Spectrum*, there must be rich insights into public discourse to warrant the production of these costly shows. While this public awareness has led to more discussion, it can result in scepticism. The 2023 exposé by the BBC's Panorama programme entitled "Private ADHD Clinics Exposed" showed ADHD clinics in the United Kingdom fast-tracking diagnosis leading to hurtful social media commentary and criticism.

Isn't everyone ADHD?

The rise of celebrity disclosure and media representation is in stark contrast with neurodivergence in the workplace. Quite simply, most people don't disclose they are neurodivergent. While many employers that I speak with have identified one or two neurodivergent evangelists within their ranks, the vast majority stay silent. This mirrors my personal experience of 20 years of silence.

I recently had the privilege of having a conversation with Marvin, who you'll hear from later in the book. Marvin and I worked together for a software firm for many years. We were a part of the same team, we travelled together, attended conferences, and spent countless hours together. Marvin's career is on a fast track, and he was recently profiled in an article as one of the top 40 people in Australian media. In reading the article, my distant pride turned to surprise when Marvin began speaking about his dyslexia, and how in his day-to-day work as a media planner he has a superpower.

At that moment I started to question why our neurodivergence was hidden from each other and the broader team. Was it pride? The pressure to conform in high-performance culture? The fear of standing out, when neurodiversity was not spoken about and didn't seem relevant to bring up? You'll hear a little more from Marvin later in the book, but (spoiler alert) it's a mixture of those things and more. For every celebrity who speaks of their newly diagnosed neurodivergence, there are millions who remain silent for reasons of their own. Throughout this book I will offer suggestions to employers, colleagues, and allies in relation to how they can make it safer and more relevant for people to speak about neurodivergence and be neurodivergent at work.

Types of neurominorities

As you build your understanding of neurodiversity it is important to acknowledge common neurominorities. Outlined below are three neurodevelopmental conditions that you are most likely to encounter in the workplace. It is important to note that co-existing, where more than one condition is present, is very common. For example, research suggests that between 50 and 70 per cent of autistic individuals present with ADHD (Hours, el al. 2022). While not covered in this book, also considered neurominorities are dyscalculia, which specifically impacts mathematical ability, and Tourette's Syndrome, characterised by involuntary movements or tics (Smith and Kirby, 2021).

We will go into these in a lot more detail in subsequent chapters; however, you may find (like me!) that you appreciate these summaries later as a succinct reference.

Autism

Definition: Autism Spectrum Disorder (ASD) is a lifelong developmental condition characterised by differences in social communication and interaction, as well as restricted and repetitive patterns of behaviour, interests, or activities (Smith and Kirby, 2021).

Prevalence: According to the World Health Organization (2023) the global prevalence of autism is estimated to be approximately 1 in 100 children. However, it's important to note that prevalence rates vary greatly across different regions, cultural groups, and between the sexes. Overall, with growing awareness and improved diagnostic techniques, the prevalence of autism is increasing. For example, one study estimated that 1 in 36 children in the United States are autistic, with boys 3.8 times more likely to be diagnosed than girls (Maenner et al., 2023).

Language: Language is hugely important and will be covered in Chapter 2. The language used to describe autism is evolving and will differ based on preference and context. Throughout this book, I use identity-first language (e.g. "autistic person"), acknowledging some prefer person-first language (e.g. "person with autism"). Autism is also associated with a number of names which can be confusing. Common terms and phrases include: ASD, "autistic", "aspie", "Aspergers", "on the spectrum", and many more. For a neurotypical manager, my advice is – if in doubt, ask the person how they would like to be referred to.

Strengths: Many autistic individuals have exceptional attention to detail, pattern recognition, and analytical thinking. They often demonstrate a unique perspective and approach to problem-solving. Autistic individuals may also exhibit a strong ability to concentrate on tasks of interest, often displaying immense passion, focus, and dedication.

Challenges: Autistic individuals may exhibit common characteristics such as difficulties in social interaction and communication. They can struggle with understanding social cues, office banter, initiating and maintaining conversations, eye contact, and interpreting nonverbal communication. Repetitive behaviours and restricted interests are also common, along with varying sensory sensitivities to sounds, lights, textures, or tastes.

Famous faces: Poet Emily Dickinson (Griffiths, 2024), Entrepreneur Elon Musk, entertainer Susan Boyle, actor Tallulah Willis (Biggs, 2024).

ADHD

Definition: Attention-Deficit/Hyperactivity Disorder (ADHD) is a lifelong developmental condition characterised by difficulties in sustaining attention, impulsivity, and hyperactivity. ADHD can impact academic, professional, and social functioning. There are three types of ADHD: 1. Predominantly hyperactive; 2. Predominantly inattentive; and 3. Combined with a blend of hyperactive and inattentive characteristics (Smith and Kirby, 2021). *I am type 1.

Prevenance: Estimates range from 2 and 7 per cent. ADHD is still underdiagnosed in most countries, particularly in girls (Smith and Kirby, 2021). As with other conditions, prevalence rates may vary.

Language: Throughout this book I use identity-first language (e.g. "ADHD person") when referring to ADHD individuals. Others may prefer person-first language (e.g. "person with ADHD"). A third variation exists, "ADHDer", which reads like a verb, perhaps because we are often on the move!

Strengths: ADHD individuals can show high levels of creativity, energy, adaptability, and out-of-the-box thinking (Smith and Kirby, 2021). Many individuals thrive in dynamic environments that require quick thinking, taking action, and multitasking.

Challenges: ADHD can present challenges related to maintaining focus, organisation, and time management. Individuals may have difficulty prioritising tasks, sustaining attention on repetitive or less interesting activities, and meeting deadlines. Impulsivity and hyperactivity can also impact social interactions and communication. Like autism, ADHD is a spectrum and presents differently in individuals (ADHD Australia, 2024).

Famous faces: Gymnast Simone Biles, entertainer Justin Timberlake, swimmer Michael Phelps, actor Mark Ruffalo (ADHD, dyslexia), and comedian Trevor Noah (ADDitude, 2023).

Dyslexia

Definition: Dyslexia is a lifelong developmental condition that effects literacy, reading, writing, and spelling (Smith and Kirby, 2021).

Prevenance: Common estimates of the prevalence of dyslexia range from 3 to 7 per cent. As with other conditions, prevalence rates may vary (Wagner et al., 2020).

Language: Throughout this book I use identity-first language (e.g. "dyslexic person") when referring to dyslexic individuals. Others may prefer person-first language (e.g. "person with dyslexia").

Strengths: Dyslexic individuals often exhibit exceptional problem-solving skills, creativity, and the ability to think outside the box. They can be resourceful, outgoing, and entrepreneurial (Smith and Kirby, 2021).

Challenges: Dyslexic individuals can experience difficulty in completing written forms. They can struggle with written communication and be slower to read information and structure written reports (Smith and Kirby, 2021).

Famous faces: Director Steven Spielberg, journalist Anderson Cooper (DeSantis, 2023) Ikea founder Ingvar Kamprad (ADHD, dyslexia) (Griffiths, 2024).

Conclusion

So, there you have it, I have attempted to cover the basics of neurodiversity and the three most common neurominorities you are likely to encounter in a workplace. I acknowledge that this is by no means a complete list. For anyone seeking further information on neurotypes, I have included recommended reading at the end of Chapter 9. In the next chapter we will cover the language of neurodiversity in some detail.

2
Why language matters

Words – so innocent and powerless as they are, as standing in a dictionary, how potent for good and evil they become, in the hands of one who knows how to combine them!

Nathaniel Hawthorne

In this chapter we will dig into the power of words, phrases, terms, and metaphors we use in everyday language at work. The aims of this chapter are to:

1. Provide an understanding of the role of inclusive language in the workplace;
2. Define common terms associated with neurodiversity; and
3. Equip leaders with tools for more effective, respectful and efficient conversations.

What's in a name? Aaron is a Hebrew name dating back thousands of years and appearing in Christian, Islamic, and Jewish texts. My name is spelled Aron with one "a". Throughout my life heretics and autocorrect frequently lead to my name being misspelt. This repeating scenario is ironic because my name was intended to be "Aaron" but was misspelt on my birth certificate. At the time, my stressed and exhausted parents didn't have access to spellcheck or have a reference book within reach. While these days I don't care and stopped correcting people sometime in the 1990s, many who realise their error are mortified. Their reaction is in stark contrast with my indifference.

I share this story as I suspect the fear of saying the wrong thing prevents us from starting the conversation about neurodivergence and disability more broadly. I have lost track of the number of times managers I speak with have become visibly frustrated or embarrassed while they stumble through language. I wonder how many more remain silent for fear of saying the wrong thing, particularly in front of colleagues, their manager, or senior leaders. Whatever the topic of discussion, no one wants to use words incorrectly or, worse still, cause offence.

While I was growing up in Australia, my grandmother instilled a love of sport in us that remains to this day. Our summers were punctuated with cricket matches and winters by the rhythm of the weekly rugby league round, while every January we would become experts in tennis for the two weeks of the Australian Open. Sports have their own vocabulary, with terms and phrases that form a cherished part of the sport itself. In some cases, sports vocabulary crosses the field of play and into everyday life. For example, audiences outside the United States that don't follow competitions like the NFL, NBA, or MBL may be familiar with phrases like "game of inches", "post season", and "stealing first base". How someone uses language when speaking about a sport provides clear evidence that they are either a true fan, an amateur supporter, or complete novice.

One recent example of the use and misuse of language happened over Christmas. While on vacation in Western Australia, I caught a ferry to Rottnest Island, seated with a group of American college students. The ferry was equipped with a TV that was broadcasting a cricket match – it was our summer, after all! Listening to the American friends grapple with and attempt to explain this foreign game was hilarious. For anyone with a basic understanding of the game, their use of language would have been the clearest evidence they had no idea what they were talking about. While our American visitors may have been a little embarrassed when corrected by local fans, I doubt they would have lost sleep over the encounter. Misuse of language in the workplace is much harder to brush off.

At work we know that language can be a powerful tool. If you have ever spent hours, days, or weeks labouring over words that express company values, or to uniquely position a product, you will know what I mean. Brands, governments, and social causes can spend millions on a single phrase that capture the unique essence of their value. Phrases like Nike's "Just Do It" or Pepsi's "The Choice of a New Generation", and Barack Obama's campaign slogan "Yes We Can" are more than mere words. When we hear these phrases they trigger a rich tapestry of associations, values, and emotions that add up to much more than the sum of their parts.

The science of language

For all the hype surrounding the computational power of generative AI we may have overlooked the supercomputer above our own shoulders. Our brains are incredibly complex and wonderful.

The average human brain contains more than 10 billion nerve cells, makes up 2 per cent of our body weight, and yet uses 20 per cent of our available energy (National Institutes of Health (US), 2007). A *New York Times* article highlighted that the average American consumes 34 gigabytes of information each day – that's a 350 per cent increase from three decades ago (Bilton, 2009). It is not surprising, then, that our brain takes shortcuts when it can. Nowhere are these shortcuts more evident than our interpretation of language.

Before we go on, some theory to help explain the power of language. Cognitive science draws on the fields of psychology, neuroscience, linguistics, and philosophy. The aim of cognitive science is to explain of how we perceive, understand, and interact with the world, often referred to as the human conceptual system. According to research the human conceptual system uses two types of information to understand the world around us: simulated and linguistic. Simulated information involves mental representations of experiences, like visualising a car or a tree when you think of one, using sensory and motor processes of the brain (Connell, 2019). Linguistic information, on the other hand, is related to the language we use, such as words and sentences that describe a car, for example.

Research suggests the average adult is exposed to 100,000 words a day (Bohn and Short, 2009 cited in Connell, 2019). Anyone in my orbit may be exposed to even more than this! This ocean of words forms complex associations in our minds to help us make sense of our world. To save energy and time, our brains rely on these associations which researchers call linguistic shortcuts. As Connell (2019, pp. 1314–15) explains, "linguistic information is available quickly and computationally cheaply, it can provide a 'quick and dirty' heuristic to determine whether it is expending precious cognitive effort on a particular conceptual processing task". So, the psychology of language explains that linguistic shortcuts are essential; they help us make sense of the world rapidly and efficiently. However, as is often the case with a shortcut, they come with a warning.

In preparing to write this book I have spent time researching how our minds work and the cognitive shortcuts or heuristics we use every day. Having no background in cognitive science, many of the concepts, while logical, were new to me, as they may be for you. When I consider the barriers to employment neurodivergent people face, systems like human bias, standard interviews, cognitive assessments, and applicant tracking systems come to mind. We will cover these barriers and suggest inclusion hacks in Chapters 4 and 5. What is clear to me now is that our own minds, through inbuilt and unconscious systems designed to save energy and time, can be unwitting barriers to inclusion. So, what can we do to at the very least be aware of the systems at play? The first step is knowing how information is presented, as specific words can heavily influence what we believe and how we act.

The power of language

The Framing effect is a cognitive bias where changes to the way information is presented impact our perceptions and decision-making. Basically, the same scenario presented with different words can be interpreted differently (Chong and Druckman, 2007). One notable example of the Framing effect is the language adopted to describe the use of illicit drugs. When you hear the phrase "the war on drugs", what image or vision comes to mind? For me, I see a newsreader, or politician in a dark suit promising to crack down on the drug epidemic or scourge.

Many researchers and advocates have expressed concerns about the use of language that dehumanises individuals caught up in the world of drugs. The language used by lawmakers, the media, and politicians to describe drug users and dealers shaped perceptions of the drug issue, particularly in America. This choice of language, laden with moral condemnation and fear, positioned drug use and distribution not just as a public health concern, but as a moral failing and a threat to societal well-being (McGinty, et al. 2019).

When it comes to how we perceive conditions such as autism and ADHD, the language has been influenced by two opposing ideological viewpoints, the medical model, and the social model of disability. The medical model views disability as a defect within the individual that requires treatment in order to function. People with disabilities often reveal frustration when met with pity or amazement if they express anything positive about their conditions (Goering, 2015).

In contrast, the social model argues that disability is the inability to participate fully in home and community life. The social model distinguishes between disabilities and impairments. Disabilities are restrictions imposed by society. Impairments are the effects of any given condition. The solution, according to this model, lies not in fixing the person, but in changing our society (Hogan, 2019). The social model of disability was first proposed by Michael (Mike) Oliver, a British sociologist with lived experience of disability. Oliver, who emphasised the importance of creating accessible environments, was an influential forerunner to the neurodiversity movement (Praslova, 2024).

The words and phrases used to describe neurodivergent people can have a powerful influence on our beliefs and actions. Even the diagnostic labels themselves are laden with negative language that influence perception. My own condition, Attention Deficit Hyperactivity Disorder, is framed in a way that emphasises the challenges. Many researchers, medical professionals, and advocates have long called for new label for ADHD, because words matter. "ADHD is an inaccurate – and potentially corrosive – name. The term 'deficit disorder' places ADHD in the realm of pathology, or disease. Individuals with ADHD do not have a disease, nor do they have a deficit of attention; in fact, what they have is an abundance of attention. The challenge is controlling it" (Hallowell and Ratey, 2024).

Now think for a minute about the way information is presented about autistic people. For example, do we describe the social or communication challenges many autistic people face in school or work? Or do we focus on autistic people's creativity, attention to detail, and honesty? The medical model of disability, in focusing on the condition and highlighting the challenges an autistic individual may face, has led to damaging, inaccurate, and frankly offensive descriptions such as "suffering from autism" or "living with autism". These descriptors and other unhelpful phrases, which we will cover later in the chapter, have no place in an inclusive workplace or society.

Inclusive language in the workplace

The dictionary definition of "inclusive language" is "language that avoids the use of certain expressions or words that might be considered to exclude particular groups of people, especially gender-specific words, such as 'man', 'mankind', and masculine pronouns, the use of which might be considered to exclude women" (Collins Dictionary, 2024).

The Diversity Council of Australia provides a useful definition of inclusive language. I find this framing easy to comprehend and incredibly empowering. Inclusive language is *effective* language – it is respectful, accurate, and relevant to all. Inclusive language is:

> *Respectful*: Inclusive language involves knowing about and showing respect for all members of a team or workplace.
>
> *Accurate*: Inclusive language gives a more accurate view of the real world by reflecting social diversity rather than perpetuating stereotypes. It avoids making false assumptions about (or stereotyping) people based on their age, cultural background, disability, gender, Indigenous background or sexual orientation and gender identity.
>
> *Relevant*: Inclusive language reflects Australia's diversity, is meaningful to a wide audience, and enables everyone to feel that they are being reflected in what is being said. To feel included, we need to "see" and "hear" ourselves reflected in the language used at work. (Diversity Council Australia, 2023

Finally, the Centre for Equity, Gender and Leadership at Berkley Hass suggests inclusive language is not about memorising a fixed list of good and bad words to use or avoid. Rather, it's about choosing compassion in how we communicate and acknowledging that context matters and language changes over time (Nee et al., 2023).

Why inclusive language in the workplace matters

We have learnt the science behind language and how the way information is presented or framed can impact our beliefs and behaviours. In workplaces today with ever-increasing pressures, who would not want to be more effective, respectful, accurate, and relevant in their communication? Think of the last challenge or conflict you faced at home or work. Did a misinterpretation, unintended offence, or inaccurate or irrelevant instructions pre-empt the situation? Under pressure, do we revert to the worst of human bias, contributing to ableism in the workplace? The use of inclusive language should not be considered as a politically correct exercise. Rather, inclusive language is a tool we can choose to adopt to be more effective, accurate, respectful, and relevant communicators. Think of the time you could save through inclusive language.

Non-inclusive language in the workplace holds many implications, including (Edith Cowan University, 2023):

- Language that is not inclusive leads to harmful stereotypes;
- Non-inclusive language affects people who witness it, as well as its targets;

- Non-inclusive language impedes the ability of excluded groups of people in the workplace, meaning they may be less likely to advance;
- Non-inclusive language can also impede certain people from ascending to leadership roles, regardless of their capability;
- Consistent non-inclusive language can be just as harmful as experiences like harassment;
- Language that is not inclusive can lead to large groups of employees feeling hostile and discriminated against.

The language we use and what is considered acceptable is dynamic and will shift over time. Terms and phrases once considered commonplace, like "blacklisted" or "chairman", are as unacceptable these days as smoking in an office. While these terms and others can still be heard, it is important to stay curious about the language you use and change with the times, be willing to learn and unlearn.

The language of neurodiversity

The language of neurodiversity is relatively new; as we learnt in Chapter 1, it dates back to Judy Singer's seminal work in 1998, with the greatest gains in awareness occurring in the last 20 years. Through this time, many have sought to offer guidance on the language of neurodiversity. Dr Nick Walker has published a body of work, firstly through an essay, Neurodiversity: Some Basic Terms & Definitions in 2014, and then through her book *Neuroqueer Heresies: Notes on the Neurodiversity Paradigm, Autistic Empowerment and*

Postnormal Possibilities (Walker, 2021). Outlined below are some basic terms and definitions and their correct use; for a detailed explanation, I encourage you to read the work of Dr Nick Walker or *The Canary Code* (Praslova, 2024).

Neurodiversity
What it means:

Neurodiversity, as we covered in Chapter 1, is a biological fact of the infinite variation in human minds, encompassing differences in cognition, emotion, and perception (Praslova, 2024).

Example of correct usage:

"Our company offers a range of assessment options, throughout the recruitment process, to accommodate the neurodiversity of our candidates" (Walker, 2014).

Examples of incorrect usage:

I have come across some baffling statements regarding neurodiversity, including: "We are looking to attract people from a neurodiversity background." This may seem like an absurd statement, but you would be surprised how often I have heard it. Another variation is "Neurodiversity point of view". Neurodiversity is neither a geographic region nor a perspective.

Neurodivergent
What it means:

Neurodivergent, an individual or individuals whose neurological functioning, communicating, and thinking differ from what are considered typical (Smith and Kirby, 2021). Neurodivergent can be abbreviated to ND (Walker, 2014). As an ADHD'er I refer to myself as neurodivergent in the workplace. Typically, when introducing myself in a meeting when it is relevant to do so, I would say I identify as neurodivergent and, depending on the setting, go on to explain I am an ADHD'er. Some people use the term neurodistinct instead of neurodivergent.

What it doesn't mean:

"*Neurodivergent* is not a synonym for autistic. There are countless possible ways to be neurodivergent, and being autistic is only one of those ways" (Walker, 2014).

Examples of correct usage:

Our company strives to be inclusive of candidates who are autistic, dyslexic, or otherwise neurodivergent.

Neurotypical
What it means:

"Neurotypical, an individual, or individuals, whose neurocognitive functioning that falls within the dominant societal standards of normal" (Praslova, 2024).

What it doesn't mean:

Neurotypical does not describe an individual, or individuals, who are non-autistic.

Examples of correct usage:

"My sister is neurotypical, but after growing up with an Autistic father and brother, she's quite at ease with other people's neurodivergence" (Walker 2014).

Neurominority
What it means:

A **neurominority or neurominority group** is a population of neurodivergent people, who all share a similar form of neuro-divergence (Praslova, 2024). Examples of neurominority groups include autistic people, dyslexic people.

Neurodiverse
What it means:

Neurodiverse is a collective term for a group that includes a combination of neurotypes. For example, a team with autistic, dyslexic, and neurotypical staff would be a neurodiverse group (Praslova, 2024).

Given that an estimated 15 per cent of the population is neuro-divergent it is highly likely that any workplace, town, or school would be neurodiverse.

What it doesn't mean:

Many people mistakenly use **neurodiverse** where the correct word would be **neurodivergent**. There is no such thing as a "neurodiverse individual". The correct term is "neurodivergent individual" (Walker, 2014).

Identity-first and person-first language – what's the difference?

Media including news, podcasts, and conferences provide a use-ful pulse check of the zeitgeist. In researching this book over the past few years, I have paid close attention to topics discussed and the way questions are phrased. Recently I have been asked numerous questions regarding the language of neurodiversity that this chapter will unpack. Regardless of how the question is phrased, I intentionally start with an explanation of identity-first and person-first language because this is a nuanced and essential aspect of promoting inclusivity and respect.

Identity-first language

Identity-first language places the condition or identity as an integral part of the individual's identity. For example, saying "autistic person" or "autistic individual" is using identity-first language (Zajic and Gudknecht, 2024). Through this book, I will use identity-first language. I preference identity-first language, respecting many of the neurodivergent individuals that I work with and including neurodivergent colleagues who prefer it. Advocates of identity-first language argue that it acknowledges the importance of the neurodivergent identity and respects the person's self-identification. It recognises that being neurodivergent is not merely a diagnosis but a fundamental aspect of a person's identity and lived experience.

One of the key advantages of identity-first language is that it empowers individuals to define themselves on their terms. It validates their identity and fosters a sense of belonging within the neurodivergent community. Many individuals and advocacy groups prefer identity-first language because they believe it reduces stigma and promotes self-acceptance. To this end, Damian Mellifont, a research fellow at the University of Sydney's Centre for Disability Research and Policy, said, "Many people who chose identity-first language saw their disability as a central part of who they were. These people don't see themselves as 'living with disability' because it's not something they carry 'with' them or can put down at the end of the day like a bag or suitcase. It's key to their identity and not something to be hidden or ashamed of" (Young, 2022).

However, it's important to note that not all neurodivergent individuals prefer identity-first language. Some may find it too defining or too closely tied to their condition, which can vary in severity and impact. This is where person-first language comes into play.

Person-first language

Person-first language separates the individual from the condition. It emphasises the person first and then acknowledges the condition as a characteristic (Zajic and Gudknecht, 2024). For instance, saying "person with autism" or "individual with ADHD" is using person-first language. Advocates of person-first language argue that it humanises the individual and avoids reducing them to their condition. One of the primary arguments for person-first language is that it focuses on the person's humanity and individuality. It can be particularly helpful when discussing medical or clinical aspects of a condition, as it places the person at the forefront of the conversation. Person-first language is often used in formal documents, clinical settings, and some educational contexts.

Navigating the choice

As you start to pay attention to this topic you will notice different language in use, and that's ok. The choice between identity-first and person-first language is deeply personal and varies among individuals. It's essential to respect the preferences of the person being described. Some individuals are vocal proponents of one approach or the other, while some may not have a strong preference.

I have spoken with hundreds of neurodivergent individuals over the years. It is worth noting that the language choice can vary depending on cultural and gender factors as well as life stage of diagnosis. What is considered respectful in one context may differ in another. Flexibility and sensitivity to individual preferences and the context of the discussion are key. As a starting point you should always "Ask the person". And when you do ask the person, don't be surprised if someone has no strong preference or language is not a topic that they are comfortable speaking about. That's ok and may also change over time, particularly if a formal or self-diagnosis is relatively new.

Ultimately, the goal is to foster inclusivity, respect, and dignity in our discussions about neurodivergence. Whichever language we choose, our intention should be to support and empower individuals and to create a more understanding and accepting workplace. What remains most crucial is respecting individuals' choices and fostering a culture of inclusion, where neurodivergent individuals are valued for their unique strengths and perspectives.

When I first started attending leadership conferences I was struck by the language of inclusion and the array of buzzwords. Words like respect, inclusion, culture, psychological safety, and so on. I would often leave these conferences informed but not sure how to put my new knowledge into practice. I am a very practical person, and a doer. My experience in speaking with neurodivergent individuals and workplaces around the world about inclusion comes down to three practical things.

1. **Ask the person** – The single biggest gain you can make is to not assume and ask the person. If you have met one neurodivergent person, you have met one neurodivergent person. We are not all the same!

2. **Drop the labels** – For every person like me who is open about their neurodivergence, know there are many more who aren't. Get to know the person first. They are much more than their diagnosis.

3. **Education** – You don't need to be an expert, but some knowledge goes a long way. The language of neurodiversity is dynamic – even individual choices may change over time so pay attention, learn, and be willing to unlearn.

In the workplace, a lack of understanding about the language of neurodiversity and how to introduce neurodivergent identity in a respectful way can be stressful for neurotypical managers. The following scenario is one I have observed that you may encounter in the workplace.

Angela's story

Angela felt anxious and unsure how to approach the conversation. A hiring manager was seeking Angela's advice about how to introduce a new team member with multiple intersecting identities. Angela's employer, a large community service organisation, had a well-established commitment to diversity, inclusion, and belonging.

Policies outlined the company's commitment to ensuring a physically and psychologically safe work environment. Senior leaders affirmed the company's diversity, inclusion, and belonging values and credentials any chance they had. And yet, Angela as Head of Human Resources did not know how to approach this situation.

Several months earlier, a programme to train and hire neurodivergent staff had launched. The company had received training from experts in the field and even established their own employee resource group with seven staff who identified as neurodivergent. Of the seven staff, Angela had only known about one, highlighting low levels of disclosure. Following a modified process, Jess had been selected for an identified position and was starting on Monday.

Through the modified recruitment process, Jess had disclosed they identify as AuADHD (autistic and ADHD). Having been diagnosed in their teens, Jess was comfortable in their neurodivergent identity and happy to share with the team. Given the recruitment process had been modified and adjustments like interview questions provided in advance, it had been necessary to disclose this. However, now, going into a team, it would be logical for Jess to think it was no longer necessary to disclose it. However, Jess's attitude was they wanted to be authentic and open, just as they were with their non-binary identity.

Did you know, autistic adults like Jess are three to six times more likely not to identify with the sex they were assigned to at birth (Warrier et al., 2020)?

The challenge was not with the new employee, Jess; it was with the established employer. The conversation Angela was dreading had nothing to do with Jess's sexual identity. The use of gender-neutral pronouns was well established. Angela did not know what to tell the anxious hiring manager, who needed advice on how to introduce their newest team member's neurodivergent identity in an inclusive way. The hiring manager had assumed that sharing Jess's autism and ADHD diagnosis was either a breach of privacy or, worse, an insult.

The situation in Angela's company is repeated regularly through workplaces around the world. In an environment where our words matter, many managers are terrified about making communication mistakes. Introducing neurodivergent identity in an inclusive way will greatly assist in the integration of neurodivergent employees, whether they are new hires, existing staff with a recent diagnosis, or moving within the organisation. It is critical to secure consent from new neurodivergent employees before sharing their identity. In Chapter 5, "Onboard and develop", I have included an onboarding email template as a resource to adapt to your own workplace.

Unhelpful language to avoid

The vast majority of managers and allies I encounter are determined to communicate respectively and use language in an inclusive way. Despite this intention, some words and phrases are unhelpful, even harmful, to fostering an inclusive environment. The words and phrases below are common and may be dismissed as harmless. However, they are anything but!

Neurodiversity word jumble. We have learnt that the language of neurodiversity is relatively new and continually evolving. As you now start to pay attention to workplace conversations, be mindful of what I call the neurodiversity word jumble. You will notice it because the person speaking may quicken the pace of their speech, mash words together and be more animated than usual. Phrases, like "neurodivergent traits" or people from a "neurodivergent background", or more recently a "neurodiversity point of view" are all misused language and can confuse an audience. Worse still, they convey a sense that the speaker does not understand what they are speaking about. Much like the American tourists talking about the game of cricket. When hearing these phrases, I am careful not to judge, rather I provide guidance on language use for further reference.

Inspiring is one word that can be used to describe people with disabilities, including neurodivergent people. Often the word is used in the context of an achievement or milestone that an individual has accomplished. Recently, I was asked to respond to the word "inspiring" while recording a podcast. While I had prepared an answer, I went off script and shared that I grind my teeth when hearing "inspiring" used to describe neurodivergent people. "Inspiring" to me indicates neurodivergent people are coming from a position of weakness, so if they have achieved anything it is in spite of their neurodivergence. Rather than thinking neurodivergent people have overcome their condition, what if their achievement was because of their neurodivergence! As one executive shared with me, their dyslexia was a gift, and they attribute their success to their neurodivergence.

Superpower is another pervasive label that I for one am guilty of promoting. In 2019 I wrote a blog titled "Is Autism a Superpower?" complete with a spiderman-inspired graphic. At the time my intention was to gain the attention of employers by highlighting skills that some autistic people possess. The blog was inspired by climate campaigner Greta Thunberg, who once said, "I have Aspergers and that means I'm sometimes a bit different from the norm. And – given the right circumstances – being different is a superpower" (Limburg, 2019). The danger of labels such as superpower and phrases like autism advantage is they place unrealistic expectations on what neurodivergent individuals can achieve. These expectations translate into an increased workload which can lead to autistic burnout, which we cover in Chapter 4.

We are all a little bit …. I have lost count of the number of times I have heard someone share that they "might have a little bit", referring to a possible but yet to be explored diagnosis. Far more pervasive and frankly damaging is the notion that we are all "on the spectrum" or we are "all a little bit". These phrases, while reducing a condition such as autism to a collection of traits, also serves to dismiss what are medically diagnosable conditions. My response if someone says they think they have or are a little bit is to be curious, not judgemental, and ask why they think that. When confronted with the catch-all "we are all a little bit", my standard response is to share that some (I am being polite, as I suspect most) neurodivergent people find that offensive. I follow this up with "I am not a little bit pregnant" to lighten the tone of the conversation.

I have often thought that neurodivergent and neurotypical people are literally speaking a different language. While sometimes these language differences can lead to harmless misunderstandings, they can have serious consequences, particularly for neurodivergent people who can interpret language literally. The following scenario is one such example.

Brad's story

Eleven weeks into his dream job Brad was exhausted. Only a few months prior Brad was thrilled, in his own unique way. His partner and family were more demonstrative in their excitement than they usually were. Brad was joining 32 graduates in the February intake for a global communications company. Brad is autistic and, like many of his neurodivergent peers, has anxiety. The graduate programme was highly competitive, so Brad chose not to disclose his autism or anxiety and had not asked for special accommodations. More accurately, Brad had seen a message about special accommodations at the bottom of the lengthy application and was initially confused by what that actually meant.

The graduate programme was by any measure professionally managed and highly regarded. It strived to be inclusive and the previous year had won an industry award for its women in STEM programme. The award had made for a great photo opportunity and pictures of the awards night were plastered around the office. The award itself, a glass trophy, was proudly displayed in a cabinet. From the outside looking in, the company was doing a lot of things right. The problem is companies don't manage; other people do that. In Brad's case his manager was professional, "thrilled to be involved in the graduate programme" and "available whenever you need anything". Brad's manager Nate was the "pick of the bunch", according to the graduate group. Nate was in his seventh year and has himself come through as a graduate. Nate's management style was encouraging, energetic, but sometimes sporadic. He liked to tell stories and use metaphors. When Brad had questions or an idea, Nate was "all ears", and that little phrase was a part of the problem. Nate had a seemingly endless vocabulary of slang phrases that took Brad some time to decipher. Brad didn't know if his colleges had the same "language barrier" and was too embarrassed to ask. Over time Brad was able to deduce the following based on trial and error and keenly observing how his team reacted:

- ***"Socialise the idea"*** *means to solicit feedback from colleagues on an idea or proposal.*

- ***"Loop back"*** *means to follow up after sharing an idea or proposal after a yet to be determined timeframe.*

- ***"Through to the keeper"*** *took a little longer to decipher. Brad was lucky to catch Nate in the office one day and noticed that while he used the phrase he gestured with his hand, as if he was waving a wand. He then turned around and said "got him" with a smile. Finally, Brad understood that this is a cricket reference and the intended meaning is to ignore the information, request, or update.*

- ***"At the end of the day ..."*** *was Nate's pet saying; he sometimes said it twice in the same breath. At first when it was used adjacent to tasks the team was undertaking – Brad thought it meant complete this by 5 p.m today.*

Many autistic people like Brad prefer direct communication that some can find insensitive or, worse still, rude. Brad would describe his communication as accurate and efficient. Brad tended to overthink scenarios and often interrupted words literally. While the use of metaphor and pet phrases maybe easy to brush off, Nate tended to provide instructions verbally, often in transit between meeting rooms, walking briskly down the hallway. Brad struggled to interrupt both Nate's words and the way they were communicated. As a part of his onboarding, Brad had requested that whenever possible instructions be provided in writing. Unfortunately, these requests were overlooked (oh, there I go, getting caught up in imprecise language). To be clearer, Brad's requests were either not being heard or were heard and ignored.

Remembering the principle of **Ask the person** discussed earlier. Nate could have asked some simple questions to understand how to get the best out of Brad and the rest of the team.

- How would you like me to communicate tasks? Verbally, via email?
- How do you like to receive feedback? Verbally, via email?
- Do you have a preferred time of the day for focused work?

When using a metaphor, pay close attention to the person's reaction. If you suspect they don't understand, ask a follow-up question, "Do you know what I mean by that?".

Scenarios like Brad's are unfortunately very common and can lead to psychological injury, burnout, productivity falls, and costly staff turnover (Brassey et al., 2022). As human resource and people managers face increased pressure to actively manage both the physical and mental well-being of neurodiverse workplaces, they would benefit from paying closer attention to language.

This chapter has covered the role of inclusive communication, defined common terms associated with neurodiversity, and provided leaders like Nate with tools for more effective, respectful, and efficient conversations. Remember that the language of neurodiversity is dynamic, and I encourage you to both listen to any neurodivergent person, their family, friends, or colleagues, and pay attention to thought leaders, some of which are listed at the end of Chapter 9.

3
Divergent in a neurotypical world

Disclaimer – Throughout this chapter more than any other in this book we will cover some confronting topics that may be triggering for some. While topics like mental health, masking, and autistic burnout are real and painful, it is important for managers and allies to be informed. If you are a neurodivergent person reading this chapter and anticipate these topics may cause distress, feel free to skip to Chapter 4. I won't tell anyone you have jumped ahead! If you choose to stick with it, at the end of this chapter I have included some well-being resources.

This chapter, "Divergent in a neurotypical world", will focus on the challenges and experiences of neurodivergent individuals and how these impact the workplace. Chapter 3 will highlight the compounding nature of challenges and how they can impact an individual's productivity, tenure, and well-being. We will acknowledge the artificial and uneven barriers placed by employers' recruitment and management practices. We will cover:

- mental health
- the legacy of school
- sleep
- masking and the impact on mental health

- autistic burnout
- managing change
- sensory environment
- employer's responsibility.

The following is an example of multiple and intersecting differences and their impact on a neurodivergent individual starting their career. Employers who adopt a one size fits all approach to attracting, recruiting, and retaining talent can overlook individuals like Ryan.

Ryan's story

The crowded foyer in the heart of the CBD was a long way from Ryan's home on the western outskirts of Sydney. Unusually for him, Ryan had woken before 8 a.m. to catch two buses and a train for today's interview. Sydney is world famous for its glittering harbour, beaches, and astronomical real estate market. But for many like Ryan, their experience is vastly different.

On first impression, Ryan looked as if he had come off the street to shelter from the searing summer heat. He was slumped on a couch, face down and scruffy. His fringe covered half of his face, he avoided eye contact like I avoid online forms. When he spoke, Ryan mumbled and looked towards the ground.

Today, Ryan had travelled into the city for his first job interview. A global logistics firm was hiring junior developers and Ryan's application had said just enough to secure him an interview. While the employer wasn't hiring based on appearance, I wondered if this was a step too far. Ryan appeared very nervous, his hands shook a little when we first met, but gradually he seemed to relax. Some candidates like Ryan relax when speaking about topics of personal interest. For this reason, I often flip an interview: rather than start with questions on work experience we cover music, cryptocurrency, and gaming. I try to keep up with Ryan. In addition to Ryan's personal interests, I discover he has a keen interest in data analytics, and after graduating from community college had taught himself to code in order to make computer games.

Interviews often focus on what is outwardly obvious. It's widely accepted that many interviewers make up their minds on a candidate in a matter of minutes (Frieder et al., 2016). A coalition of biases can result in interviewers favouring candidates who look, speak, and act like them. Ryan may as well have come from another planet, many would not give him a chance. Despite his mumbled responses and terrible shoes, Ryan secured an interview and was offered a role with the firm. In his own way Ryan was excited. When I rang him to say a contract was being issued his understated response was priceless, he simply said, "sweet".

When first meeting someone it is hard to understand the compounding layers of disadvantage that many neurodivergent people face. Ryan was diagnosed with autism and ADHD at school; he wouldn't share much but it was clear that he had some trauma from this time. Families of autistic children are more likely to earn insufficient income and experience parental divorce (Hoover, Kaufman, 2018). It is hardly surprising that an estimated 70 per cent of autistic people have an associated mental health condition, such *as anxiety or depression (World Economic Forum, 2022). Through the application process, Ryan had shared that he has anxiety.*

Now, as a young adult living in a single-parent household, Ryan was not able to work full time as he needed to support his mum and younger siblings. He also lived 90 minutes from the office. Ryan didn't drive and would need to take two buses and a train to make it to work. It was pre-Covid and the world has not yet embraced hybrid working. In situations like these, employers who provide flexibility with hours and working from home can change lives for the better. Ryan started three days a week and the early reports where he was a fast learner and asked good questions.

Two months into Ryan's tenure, I received a worried call from Jade, who managed onboarding of staff through Asia Pacific. The call had nothing to do with Ryan's performance, from what I had been told he was ahead of schedule in his induction. There were no concerns about his appearance, reduced hours, or remote working. In fact, Ryan had been offered shares in the company through the company's employee share scheme. However, to the amazement of everyone, Ryan had rejected the offer. Out of 1800 local employees, only one person had ever opted out, and it was Ryan. The shares were a standard part of the company's compensation package, issued over and above salary as a bonus to all.

The conversation with Jade went something like this. "Aron, it's a no brainer, I can't fathom why anyone would reject this offer." The shares are vested over 12 months, they are a bonus on top of salary. It was assumed that Ryan must be *unhappy in his role and looking elsewhere, why else would he reject a $10,000 bonus?*

I said I would call Ryan to find out what was going on. "One thing, though, Jade, Ryan may not understand what terms like equity and vesting mean. I'll come back to you." It tuns out my hunch was correct; Ryan had no idea what a share was or what he could do with it. I broke it down to basics; the company is listed on the Stock Exchange, meaning thousands of people own small pieces of it. All staff are offered a small piece of the company they are helping grow; if you don't wish to keep the shares they can be easily sold. If you accept the offer, you can do what you want with the additional $10,000. Explained like this, the decision was indeed a no-brainer.

While the tale ended with Ryan receiving his bonus shares, a combination of factors led to the initial rejection. Aside from a lack of financial literacy, Ryan has a limited social network to seek counsel from. No one in his small family and friends circle has a share portfolio, many are surviving payday to payday. The announcement on the employee share scheme was made during an in-person town hall meeting during which Ryan was often anxious. Ryan's anxiety during in-person meetings means he often fails to take in important information. Finally, the written information about the employee share scheme was longer than an airport novel. The guide was littered with financial jargon which could have baffled anyone but an avid investor.

In a different workplace, with a less curious manager, Ryan could have easily missed out on what for him was a significant sum of money.

In hindsight, a few simple steps could have prevented what was ultimately a misunderstanding.

1. For the company-wide announcement, offer this through in-person and virtual options.
2. Supplement the guide with a two-page jargon-free summary.
3. Don't assume a level of financial literacy, especially for new employees in their first role.
4. Be curious, not judgemental, when questions arise.
5. As covered in Chapter 2, ask the person!

Ryan's story highlights the nuanced, intersecting, and compounding nature of disadvantage many neurodivergent people face: co-existing mental health; social isolation; economic disadvantage; lack of professional network; single-parent households.

It is important for employers to be aware of the challenges and alive to the skills and unique perspectives while actively supporting neurodivergent staff. The following section will cover some of the challenges neurodivergent individuals face, including: mental health, past trauma from school, sleep disturbances, masking, autistic burnout, managing change, and cogitative rigidity and the sensory environment. Neuroinclusive employers need to be aware of these challenges and provide appropriate support.

Mental health

Starting my career in the early 2000s, at a time before smartphones and social media, mental health was largely absent from the conversation about workplace safety. The prevailing attitude was to toughen up and get the job done. I remember once attending and trying my best to sit through a workplace health and safety seminar. The topics covered included tripping hazards in the office and paying attention when walking from the meals room with hot beverages. It was hard to stay focused! The risks were all obvious and, more importantly, visible. I do appreciate there are many workplaces, such as those in the construction industry, transport industry, and those of first responders, where risks are more significant. The workplace risks impacting mental health are less visible, more costly, and increasingly are coming to the attention of business leaders around the world.

The prevalence of mental health conditions has been rising over the decades, influenced by several factors such as increased awareness, reduced stigma, and improved diagnostics. Mental health disorders such as anxiety and depression are very common. The World Health Organization estimates 1 in every 8 people, or 970 million people around the world, are living with a mental disorder (World Health Organization, 2022). Covid-19 led to a 25 per cent surge in anxiety and depression. Around the globe millions struggled with pandemic-related stress such as social isolation from lockdowns, financial worries, and fear of infection (World Health Organization, 2022). I have spoken with dozens of neurodivergent people who have received a diagnosis in the last two years, and reported that the stress and change to routine during Covid-19 lockdowns led to a diagnosis.

Neurodivergent workers are more likely to impacted by mental health. Several studies have indicated that neurodivergent people have a greater vulnerability to developing mental health issues through their lifetime from adolescence into adulthood

(Accardo et al., 2022; Kirby, 2021). Neurodivergent individuals can face unique challenges in the workplace impacting mental health. Autistic employees may experience sensitivity to sensory inputs like bright lights or loud noises, leading to increased stress and anxiety. They might also struggle with workplace communication and unstructured social interactions. Australia's Draft National Autism Strategy noted that autistic people are 2.5 times more likely to experience depression than the general population (Department of Social Services, 2024). ADHD'ers can struggle with executive functioning skills such as time management, organisation, and sustaining attention on tasks. Doyle (2020) cited in Zindell (2024) argues that mental health needs can be the consequence of an unsupported neurominority. An individual who is frustrated, excluded, and unable to reach their potential is likely to feel anxious or depressed.

The legacy of school

School can be the best of times and the worst of times. While this book focuses on the workplace, it must be recognised that today's workers were yesterday's students. For many neurodivergent people, myself included, school could and can be challenging.

The industrial model of education, with its standardised curriculum and assessment methods, often fails to accommodate the diverse learning styles of neurodivergent students. According to some studies, 77 per cent of autistic students experience bullying at school, a rate much higher than their neurotypical peers (Cappadocia et al., 2012). As a result, autistic and neurodivergent students can experience higher rates of bullying, absenteeism, and mental health challenges (Cappadocia et al., 2012). As employers seeking to understand neurodivergent candidates they are interviewing, or staff currently employ, a good starting point is to acknowledge the likelihood of historical trauma that neurodivergent employees may have experienced though school.

Sleep disturbances

Many people struggle to get a good night's sleep. Neurodivergent people are more likely than their neurotypical peers to experience sleep disturbances. These disturbances can include a delay in falling asleep, waking multiple times, difficulty returning to sleep, and less duration of sleep. Research has shown that up to 85 per cent of ADHD individuals have difficulties falling or staying asleep (Zhu et al., 2023). Autistic adults experience worse sleep quality than non-autistic adults. Poor sleep contributes to worsened quality of life as well as decreased mental and physical wellbeing (McLean et al., 2021).

Employers who offer flexible scheduling can enable employees to adjust their work hours to better align with their individual needs. I have worked for years with several neurodivergent colleagues with sleep disturbances. Everyone has their own operating rhythm, with many starting later in the day and working into the early evening. Personally, I am up at 5 a.m. each day and seldom work late into the afternoon. Our team overlaps for six hours each day, from 10 a.m. to 4 p.m. To accommodate the needs of our neurodivergent team, no meetings are scheduled before 10 a.m. or after 4 p.m. Not all employers have this flexibility, but it has worked for us. The benefit of flexible start times is we can cover an extended workday, from 7 a.m. to 6 p.m. So, the sleep disturbances of some, combined with a flexible approach to when and how work is done, are positively contributing to productivity.

Masking and the impact on mental health

Masking, or camouflaging, refers to the practice of neurodivergent individuals, particularly autistics, altering their behaviour to conform to neurotypical standards (Hull et al., 2017). This includes suppressing stimming (self-stimulating) behaviours, forcing eye contact, or mimicking social cues. I have spoken with several autistic individuals who have taught themselves to laugh along with jokes while not finding anything funny. Others have reported writing down a list of small-talk questions to ask colleagues in preparation for a work function and then practising the delivery.

We are all taught to modify our behaviour to suit certain social situations. We are likely, for example, to eat a meal differently if seated at a function with strangers compared to eating on the couch with friends or family. However, most of us don't require our dinner function persona all the time. For neurodivergent people, while masking can facilitate social interactions, it comes at a significant mental health cost. The effort to constantly monitor and adjust behaviour can lead to increased stress, anxiety, and depression (Miller et al., 2021).

Autistic burnout describes a condition experienced by autistic individuals due to chronic life stress, a mismatch of expectations and abilities, and a lack of adequate support. Raymaker et al., 2020) described autistic burnout as experiences of chronic exhaustion, increased sensitivity to sensory input, diminished social skills, and a sense of losing their abilities to manage daily tasks. It is not uncommon for autistic burnout to last for weeks or months. Some autistic individuals I have spoken with have experienced symptoms for years. Prolonged burnout can be devasting for professional, personal relationships, finances, as well as physical and mental wellbeing.

Managing change

Change is the new constant in today's workplaces. Restructures, acquisitions, as well as changes to remote hybrid or office working conditions can be especially challenging for neurodivergent people to manage. Several neurodivergent individuals I spoke with acknowledged they were slow to embrace change and can struggle to grasp others point of view. Resistance to change can be attributed to neurodivergent traits such as:

Cognitive rigidity: Some neurodivergent, particularly autistic, individuals may exhibit cognitive rigidity, which refers to a resistance to change in thinking or behaviour. This rigidity can make it challenging for them to adapt to new ways of doing things or to consider alternative perspectives, leading to resistance or anxiety in the face of change (Petrolini et al., 2023).

Executive functioning challenges: Many neurodivergent individuals, including ADHD'ers like me, may experience difficulties with executive functioning, which includes skills such as planning, organising, and transitioning between tasks. Changes in workflow or procedures can disrupt their established routines and strategies, leading to increased stress and difficulty in adapting.

Difficulty with unpredictability: Some neurodivergent individuals thrive on predictability and routine. Changes in work processes, team dynamics, or expectations can introduce uncertainty and unpredictability, which can be overwhelming for individuals who rely on structure and predictability to manage their tasks and responsibilities.

Sensory environment

Sensory sensitivities can profoundly affect neurodivergent individuals in the workplace. It is in this environment where unexpected noises, bright lights, or even the office ambiance can be distracting or overwhelming – as I found in a meeting, detailed in the following scenario.

George Street

George Street, Sydney, wouldn't be the first place I would choose for a business meeting. Perpetual construction, trams gliding past, and almond milk frothing at numerous cafés. There are hundreds of people in my view, all rushing somewhere. I try to focus on my meeting preparation and jot down a few notes. I am meeting a close supporter of our work in the government sector to get a first-hand account of what is happening, or, more accurately, what is not happening. The challenge I am seeking to overcome is a lack of hiring managers volunteering to take on neurodivergent graduates. This is not unusual, I have spoken to organisations committed to employment inclusion in the US, Canada, India, South Korea, Netherlands, and Italy all with similar challenges. Public commitments by corporate and government leaders that are not matched by results in jobs for neurodivergent people. Jim greets me warmly and we order.

Coffees arrive, the meeting starts, and we bounce ideas off each other. As a starting point we agree that the foundations are all in place. The department has a multi-year transformation project it is struggling to deliver due to chronic skills shortages. The previous summer the state government made a public commitment to increasing the representation of people with disabilities. The following year, managers and staff received training on neurodiversity inclusion.

Jim suggests that suitable candidates are being overlooked after failing the interview. He can think of dozens of cases where the skills of a candidate represented on paper were not evident in the interview. I remind Jim that many neurodivergent individuals, particularly autistics, struggle with verbal interviews. Jim continues, he thinks the sterile office environment of the department headquarters is contributing to candidates' nerves. The new headquarters, I am told, will be bright and open plan, but that move is still 18 months away. Something needs to change right now.

Suddenly, an idea! When performance conversations are needed Jim has found some team members relax when taken out of the office for a coffee. What if interviews could be conducted here? Jim announces that he will start doing interviews with candidates at the very café we are sitting at. My response both surprises and deflates Jim; I simply say, "please don't". When pressed on why this approach to interviewing candidates won't work, I decide to go off script.

"Well Jim, you know I am neurodivergent. I am sitting here trying my best to listen and contribute to this conversation. I sometimes struggle to maintain focus on things that do not interest me, such as tax returns, directions to the station, or voicemail messages. But this is a conversation I am very interested in and yet here is what I am also thinking about while we have been speaking … How long has Sydney had trams again? Construction took years, it was strange seeing George Street ripped up … Mum told me when she was a girl they had trams to Bondi, that would be cool … Hey, is that Chris I played rugby with? Wow, he has put on some weight. Another tram passes and there is an ad for the new Marvel movie, which one is that in the series? Should I catch up on the other movies before watching that one? Are my sons old enough for a Marvel movie? Empire Strikes Back *was the first movie I saw at the cinema, walking back to the car I thought there were stormtroopers in the side streets …." I finish my monologue and confess that those thoughts are from the past two minutes, Jim doesn't say a word.*

Jim was not your typical manager. Over years Jim has researched neurodiversity, participated in multiple training sessions covering sensory challenges and social anxiety, and mentored neurodivergent people. Yet despite this Jim can't betray his own heuristics. Rather than assuming what works in the context of performance discussions will work with candidates in a job interview, Jim could co-design an approach with the neurodivergent staff he mentors. Or simply ask the question with his neurodivergent staff, "Would a job interview in a café work for you?".

In my work advising employers on neuroinclusion, the physical setting of the workplace is a common area of intervention. Where interviews take place matters. High-sensory environments can be kryptonite for neurodivergent people, those with sensory sensitivities or social anxiety. For neurodivergent individuals, high-sensory environments can be overwhelming and distressing. Sensory processing issues are common characteristics of many neurodivergent conditions. These individuals may have heightened sensitivity to sounds, lights, and other sensory stimuli that most people find tolerable (Praslova, 2024). In a busy café, the constant chatter, clinking of glasses, and music can be overwhelming and cause sensory overload, leading to anxiety and difficulty concentrating. I have found this to be true for myself having struggled for years in "off site" meetings that are intended to create a more relaxed atmosphere and break up the day.

This sensory overload can have a significant impact on performance in an interview or meeting, where it is essential to be able to concentrate, process information quickly, and communicate effectively. However, for someone who is struggling to process sensory input, these tasks become much more challenging. Neurodivergent people may struggle to focus on the interviewer's questions or to articulate their thoughts clearly, leading to a poor performance. In addition to the sensory challenges, environments like cafés can also be socially overwhelming for neurodivergent individuals. Many neurodivergent people struggle with social interaction, particularly in unfamiliar situations. In a café setting, there are often numerous distractions and interruptions that can make it difficult to maintain focus on the interviewer or to pick up on social cues. This can lead to a breakdown in communication and further exacerbate the individual's anxiety and stress.

All of these factors can lead to poor interview or meeting performance and, ultimately, unfavourable employment outcomes for neurodivergent individuals. The inability to perform well in an interview can limit their opportunities for employment and make it difficult to advance in their careers.

Employer's responsibility

Employers I speak with are aware of their responsibility to maintain both a physically and psychologically safe workplace. HR professionals and senior leaders are under pressure to deliver positive duty actions; proactive steps are needed to identify risks and support employees' mental health. These actions are driven partly by the realisation that poor mental health is costly; employees grappling with poor mental health are more likely to have higher rates of absenteeism, reduced productivity, and decreased engagement at work. It is estimated that depression and anxiety cost the global economy an estimated US$1 trillion annually in lost productivity (Chodavadia et al., 2023).

Several developed countries, including Australia, the United Kingdom, and Canada, have begun to codify the responsibility of maintaining a psychologically safe workplace within their workplace safety legislation. Employers in these countries and many others now have a legal as well as moral and business imperative to actively manage mental health.

How can you support neurodivergent employee's mental health?

Many employers are unfamiliar with the unique workplace triggers that impact upon the mental health of neurodivergent people. What is more, employers don't have accurate employee data. Quite simply, they don't realise who is neurodivergent. The same goes for other invisible disabilities, and this extends to chronic health conditions.

We will cover the link between disclosure and belonging in Chapter 7 as I believe it's a critical part of workplace inclusion. For now, it's important to realise that employers face a challenge of being responsible for maintaining a physically and psychologically safe workplace while not knowing which employees maybe at increased risk.

Neurodivergent employees often face workplace triggers such as:

- Active or casual discrimination;
- Bullying continuing from school into the workplace;
- Communication challenges;
- Frequent changes to tasks and priorities;
- Poorly communicated changes;
- Lack of flexibility in how and where work is done;
- Stress of conforming to neurotypical standards; and
- Sensory environment

In the following chapters I will introduce practical interventions that neuroinclusive leaders can employ to mitigate workplace risks.

Conclusion

In Chapter 2 we heard of Brad and his challenges with the communication style of manager, Nate. In this scenario, the overuse of metaphor, Nate's tendency to provide instructions verbally despite requests for written communication, and constant changes to priorities were all triggers for Brad that negatively impacted his mental health. Unfortunately, it is not uncommon for this scenario to result in employees requiring medical treatment, including hospitalisation.

Through this chapter we have covered the nuanced, intersecting, and compounding nature of disadvantage that many neurodivergent employees can face. Collectively, these challenges effect how neurodivergent people experience work and employers need to understand and actively manage workplace triggers. The challenge for employers is that many lack transparent data on neurodivergent employees.

Well-being resources

For those struggling with mental health, there is help available. Here is a selection of organisations that offer support for mental health challenges, some of which have specific resources or understanding of neurodiversity:

Australia

- Beyond Blue: Offers support for Australians to achieve their best possible mental health, including resources and helplines for anxiety, depression, and suicide prevention. Website: **beyondblue.org.au**

- SANE Australia: Provides support, training, and education enabling those with a mental illness to lead a better life. Website: **sane.org**

Canada

- CAMH (Centre for Addiction and Mental Health): Canada's largest mental health teaching hospital, offering services for mental health and addiction. Website: **camh.ca**
- Mood Disorders Society of Canada (MDSC): Dedicated to providing information, education, and support to individuals with mood disorders, including those that may intersect with neurodiversity. The MDSC works to improve access to treatment, inform research, and reduce stigma through advocacy and education. Their resources can be valuable for neurodivergent individuals facing mental health challenges. Website: **mdsc.ca**

Hong Kong

- Mind Hong Kong (Mind HK): Committed to improving awareness and understanding of mental health in Hong Kong. They provide resources, support, and advocacy to destigmatise mental health issues. Website: **mind.org.hk**
- The Samaritans Hong Kong: Provides confidential emotional support to anyone who is suicidal or in emotional distress. Their services are available 24/7 and are free of charge. While they primarily serve the local population, they can assist English speakers. Website: **samaritans.org.hk**

India

- The Live Love Laugh Foundation: Focuses on giving hope to every person experiencing stress, anxiety, and depression. Website: **thelivelovelaughfoundation.org**

- MPower: Aims to stamp out stigma and create a society that talks about mental health openly. Website: **mpowerminds. com**

Ireland

- Mental Health Ireland: Promotes positive mental health and well-being to all individuals and communities, and supports people who experience mental health challenges. Website: **mentalhealthireland.ie**
- Aware: Offers support for people affected by stress, depression, bipolar disorder, and mood-related conditions in Ireland. They provide a range of services including support groups, a support line, and education programmes. Website: **aware.ie**

New Zealand

- Mental Health Foundation of New Zealand: Provides free information and training, and advocates for policies and services that support people with experience of mental illness. Website: **mentalhealth.org.nz**
- I AM HOPE: Offers youth mental health support and advocacy. Website: **iamhope.org.nz**

Singapore

- SAMH (Singapore Association for Mental Health): Offers a range of mental health services and public education efforts. Website: **samhealth.org.sg**
- Silver Ribbon (Singapore): Promotes positive attitudes towards mental health and provides support for those affected by mental health issues. Website: **silverribbonsingapore.com**

United Kingdom

- Mind: Offers information and support for anyone facing a mental health problem. Website: **mind.org.uk**
- National Autistic Society: Provides support and resources not just for autistic individuals but can be helpful for neurodivergent people more broadly. Website: **autism.org.uk**

United States

- NAMI (National Alliance on Mental Illness): The nation's largest grassroots mental health organisation dedicated to building better lives for the millions of Americans affected by mental illness. Website: **nami.org**
- ADAA (Anxiety and Depression Association of America): Focuses on the prevention, treatment, and cure of anxiety, depression, OCD, PTSD, and co-occurring disorders. Website: **adaa.org**

These organisations offer various forms of support, including hotlines, counselling services, informational resources, and advocacy, which can be especially helpful for neurodivergent individuals facing mental health challenges, both personally and professionally.

To find mental health resources in countries not covered, you can use a targeted Google search that combines specific keywords related to mental health support with the country of interest. Here's a general template for an efficient search term: "mental health resources" + [Country Name] + "support" + "neurodiversity" or "neurodivergent".

If required, I hope you get the support you need.

In the chapter to follow, I will introduce the employment lifecycle and will focus on the first two stages of attraction and recruitment, while discussing implications for neurodivergent employees. See you there!

4
Inclusion through the employee lifecycle – attract and recruit

As we explore neuroinclusion through the employee lifecycle, it is important to consider what interventions are possible at each stage. Cattermole (2019) identifies six stages of the employee lifecycle, each presenting an opportunity for neuroinclusion. The stages of the employee lifecycle are outlined in Table 1 below. For consistency I will adopt the same stages throughout as I proceed to discuss practical and inclusive ways of improving employment prospects for neurodivergent people.

Table 1. Stages of the employee lifecycle

1. **Attract:** A potential applicant learns of the organisation and forms opinions about whether they would be interested in working there.
2. **Recruit:** Candidates move through the search and hiring process, including job ads, CV screening, and interviews.

3. **Onboard:** New employees are brought into the organisation and trained.
4. **Develop:** Employees enhance their skills and advance their careers within the organisation through additional learning and development.
5. **Retain and advance:** Employees are encouraged to remain and advance in the organisation through various organisational practices, such as offering benefits, additional training, and promotion.
6. **Separate:** Employees either move to another organisation or retire and are offboarded.

(Cattermole, 2019)

We have reached the point where theory meets practice. This chapter covers practical actions employers can take to attract and recruit neurodivergent individuals. Also included are workplace hacks that may sound trivial but, when implemented, can make a significant difference. As I press ahead, it's time to turn these insights into action. This transition raises important questions. For instance, what does a neuroinclusive hiring process look like? Also, how can managers foster a culture that doesn't just accommo-date but celebrates neurodivergent talents? The chapter will dis-cuss the attract and recruit stages of the employment lifecycle and what these mean in terms of advancing diversity and inclusion. The chapter concludes with questions hiring and talent managers can ask to critically evaluate their recruitment process.

Attract

Several employers I have spoken with lament the lack of diverse talent applying for their positions. Whether the intent is to increase hiring of women, culturally diverse or neurodivergent applicants, it is common to blame the pipeline, while not considering the channels used to attract applications. As Rivera (2012) argued, employers believe that the diversity of their workforce is a pipeline issue, yet they typically draw from a very narrow pool of elite schools. Rivera's study explained, "Firms are scrambling for diversity. They want gender diversity, racial diversity, you name it, and [they] go to great lengths to attract diverse applicants. They are all fighting for the same tiny piece of the pie. But they are focusing on that slice rather than expanding it, which is the real problem" (Rivera, 2012, p.78).

Neuroinclusive leaders take deliberate steps to look for candidates outside traditional channels, such as online advertising like Indeed, Seek, and Glassdoor, as well as social platforms including LinkedIn and Facebook. As Tania Martin from EY put it in the "Neurodiversity with Theo Smith' podcast, I don't want to interview the candidate who would typically apply for a job at EY. I want to find the people who would not typically apply (Smith, 2024).

Skewed job ad visibility can limit an employer's chance of attracting diverse candidates. Neuroinclusive leaders like auticon engage with a wide range of candidate attraction channels as a way of connecting with neurodivergent candidates that traditional advertising can miss, including:

- Universities, especially, Student Support Services
- Community Organisations
- Not-for-Profits who focus on Autism, ADHD and Dyslexia
- Neurodiversity Employment Organisations

- Social media influences who focus on Autism, ADHD and Dyslexia
- Online communities
- Friends and family of existing neurodivergent consultants.

To be successful, an employer will need to test multiple channels of candidate attraction and closely monitor acquisition metrics. If you are hiring, why not test one new channel from the list above?

Advertising and job descriptions

Here is a task, the next time you look at a job description, count how many pages it encompasses. I once took a brief from a corporate employer hiring software testers, sometimes called Test Engineer, or QA. The hiring manager was able to explain to me in plain language what the role entailed in the time it took to reach the elevator after our meeting. To my surprise the following day a seven-page job description landed in my inbox. The role requirements took up a full page! The employer's value proposition and equal opportunity statements covered another two. Several hundred words, covering what the hiring manager had managed to articulate in under a minute the day before.

Many neuroinclusive leaders have either ditched the job description entirely or at the least radically rethought it. At Xceptional we found one of the quickest wins was placing a percentage of time estimate against each task. This was in response to several neurodivergent candidates querying the importance of tasks required for the role. Importantly we understand you can't predict the future, so we emphasise these percentage estimates, are exactly that, estimates.

Below is an example of a job description for a Talent Acquisition Manager.

Job Title: Talent Acquisition Manager

Company Overview:

Xceptional is an award-winning social enterprise committed to creating inclusive employment opportunities for neurodivergent individuals. As experts in neurodivergent employment, our training and consulting guides employers in building sustainable organisational cultures.

Job overview:

We are seeking an experienced Talent Acquisition Manager to lead and oversee our recruitment efforts for neurodivergent candidates and employer partners. The successful candidate will be responsible for sourcing, screening, and selecting candidates who demonstrate the necessary skills and potential to thrive in a variety of roles.

Requirements:

- At least five years of experience in recruitment, with a focus on diversity and inclusion;
- Knowledge and understanding of neurodiversity and the unique needs and strengths of neurodivergent individuals;
- Proven track record of successfully sourcing candidates for a variety of roles;
- Strong communication and interpersonal skills;

- Strong organisational and time management skills;
- Ability to work independently and collaboratively as part of a small team; and
- Ideally located in Brisbane, Melbourne, or Sydney.

Responsibilities:

- Leverage existing and develop new recruitment strategies to attract a diverse pool of neurodivergent candidates (20%);
- Source candidates through a variety of channels, including job boards, social media, and community organisations (20%);
- Conduct initial screenings of candidates to assess fit for open positions (15%);
- Work with hiring managers to understand their needs and requirements for open positions (15%);
- Schedule and coordinate interviews with candidates and hiring managers (15%);
- Collaborate with the Xceptional team to ensure a smooth and efficient recruitment process (10%); and
- Track and report on recruitment metrics to measure the effectiveness of recruitment strategies (5%).

It's important to note that these percentages are estimates and may vary depending on the specific needs and priorities of the company.

Benefits:

- Competitive salary with not-for-profit salary packaging;

- Flexible work schedule and remote work options;
- A supportive and inclusive work environment that values diversity and individuality; and
- Opportunity to make a meaningful impact in the lives of neurodivergent individuals and contribute to a more inclusive society.

We encourage individuals who identify as neurodivergent to apply for this position, as we are committed to creating a workplace that is welcoming and supportive of all individuals.

To encourage neurodivergent applicants to first read your job description and better still apply, commit to flexibility as suggested by Smith and Kirby (2021). Throughout the recruitment process, including job advertising consider adding the following wording:

> 'We encourage neurologically diverse applications from all backgrounds, so is there anything we can do to make this process better for you and to allow you to show your best self'?

Furthermore, you could consider adding this wording:

> 'We recognise that some people require extra time to complete tests or require alternative methods of presentation and can benefit from having the interview questions or a guide to the type of questions pre-interview. We are open to any suggestions or requests you might have and are always looking for creative ways to assist' (Smith and Kirby, 2021, p.116).

Recruit

As we continue to explore neuroinclusion through the employee lifecycle our attention turns to the critical stage of recruitment. Do you enjoy job interviews? If you are comfortable speaking about your achievements, quickly establishing rapport and creatively answering questions, then an interview will play to your strengths. However, for many neurodivergent candidates, the traditional recruitment process, including pre-employment assessments and job interviews are especially challenging to navigate (Davies et al., 2023). Many autistic people struggle with social skills, maintaining eye contact and verbal communication, making an interview close to the perfect situation to show an autistic adult at their worst. ADHD'ers can be prone to overthinking, disorganisation and impulsivity which can impact their success in job interviews (Kash, 2021). Dyslexic candidates face barriers in pre-employment through aptitude tests and written applications. Wissell et al. (2022) noted that participants felt unable to show their employability to prospective employers and raised this as a barrier to gaining certain jobs.

Tailored recruitment processes

All neuroinclusion leaders have modified or scrapped standard recruitment processes to accommodate the unique needs of neurodivergent individuals. This includes providing clear job descriptions, providing work samples to better assess the actual skills of the candidates, allowing extra time for tasks, or modifying interview techniques, and offering alternatives to standard interviews to reduce anxiety. Tania Martin, EY's Neuro-Diverse Centre of Excellence leader in the UK, has built on the early work of her colleagues in the US. In a podcast interview with Theo Smith, Tania shared how EY "set about ripping up the rule book concerning how we approach recruitment". EY have since adopted an "anti-recruitment" process where neurodivergent candidates are screened in rather than out (Smith, 2024).

There are four steps in EY's modified recruitment process. It was a surprise to me that everyone who applies for the programme gets an interview. In fact, all applicants for the programme progress through three stages. Critically, they are given the chance to build confidence in progressing through these stages. Not everyone gets a job, but they get a chance to demonstrate their skills through tailored work trials.

Similarly, Microsoft developed a hiring process that includes multiple stages that focus on work trials and team projects rather than conventional interviews. This approach allows candidates to demonstrate their skills in an environment similar to the actual workplace. As Mensik explains, "The non-traditional interview format helps better gauge candidates' potential performance rather than their behaviours" (Mensik, 2024). Microsoft provides clear communication on the programme in multiple formats. The programme's webpage contains videos, clear text, bullet points. The webpage layout is uncomplicated with a plain white background, and limited images. That's it, no waffle about the company's employer value proposition, just facts about what applicants can expect and stories of neurodivergent people employed through the programme. The webpage also includes a four-minute video which explains the process in detail, while text subtitles display automatically to cater for applicants with differences in verbal processing.

The tailored recruitment process adopted by EY and Microsoft is backed by research. A 2023 study compared autistic, neurodivergent, and neurotypical adults' experiences of hiring processes in the UK (Davies et al., 2023). The study concluded that autistic and neurodivergent participants had fewer positive experiences with traditional interviews, group tasks, and psychometric tests. Interestingly, the study identified similarities between neurodivergent and neurotypical experience, including the perceived need for more flexible recruitment methods and a desire for more clarity surrounding the hiring process and what to expect (Davies et al., 2023).

Recruitment in the age of AI

Few business practices have benefited more from technology than recruitment. As Nikolaou (2021) explains, "in recruitment and selection, technology has affected the whole recruitment and selection lifecycle". Many researchers, industry leaders, and commentators claim that the use of recruitment technology tools like Applicant Tracking Systems level the playing field for diverse applicants. Several studies have concluded that standardised tests and a uniform process provide the best opportunity for employers to assess relevant skills and candidates to progress based on merit. For example, Hunkenschroer and Luetge (2022) argue "data-driven assessment leads to hiring of 'nontraditional' candidates who might typically not make it through a hiring process (e.g. from a non-elite college, but with other strong skills)".

Few technologies have captured attention like generative AI. Tools like ChatGPT, Copilot, and Gemini are weaving their way into every aspect of work and home life. Advocates of AI claim the technologies hold great promise for eliminating bias and increasing workforce diversity (Polli, 2019). However, as with any technology or business tool, there are potential risks. Researchers and diversity advocates have raised concerns about systematic bias through AI (Hunkenschroer and Luetge, 2022). Data scientist Cathy O'Neil sounded the alarm on the use of mathematical models or algorithms in her book *Weapons of Math Destruction*. O'Neil identifies risks in the use of recruitment technologies where "human resource departments rely on automatic systems to winnow down piles of resumes. In fact, some 72% of resumes are not seen by human eyes" (O'Neil, 2016, pp. 113–114). She argues that recruitment algorithms often perpetuate existing human biases, leading to discriminatory hiring practices, now at an industrial scale.

As inclusive leaders, there are opportunities to work alongside recruitment technology. If your workplace uses technology such as standardised tests and applicant tracking systems, you could adopt an experimental approach to gauge who you may be missing out on as follows:

- Identify a role you would like more diverse applicants for;
- Select ten applicants who are to be screened;
- Offer a work sample to these ten applicants instead of an interview; and
- Determine if any of the ten applicants' work sample assessment justifies an interview.

If the experiment is a success, repeat twice more and then consider how you can adapt your current process to screen in a wider pool of candidates.

What stage am I up to?

Have you ever found yourself in the middle of a recruitment process and had no idea what stage you are up to? I certainly have, and it adds to the stress of the recruitment experience. Not knowing what to expect from the start or how you are progressing is challenging for both neurodivergent and neurotypical candidates. Transparency of the role requirements, the steps of the recruitment process, as well as evaluation criteria, will reduce stress for neurodivergent and neurotypical candidates as well as the talent and hiring managers. Unfortunately, many recruitment processes are about as clear as mud.

As Davies argues, "uncertainty and ambiguity that pervade in all aspects of the recruitment process. Indeed, ambiguity was felt to be an issue right from the start of the hiring process with many participants noting that job specifications often name vague, generic skills" (Davies et al., 2023, p. 1756).

Markel and Elia (2006) suggest transparency in the recruitment process and how roles are advertised is critical to attract autistic and neurodivergent applicants. Job descriptions and advertisements need to include simple, easy-to-understand language that covers the job duties and how to apply.

What can employers do?

- Provide clear instructions on what candidates can expect at each step.

- Include a simple one-page guide on the recruitment process detailing the steps.
- Assign a single point of contact to lead applicants through the process.
- Include photos of your office and those conducting interviews to reduce anxiety.
- Provide clear instructions of dress code; don't assume the candidate knows.
- Offer detailed instructions on the interview location, whether it is physical or virtual.
- Offer personalised feedback after each stage.

As a guide, the talent or HR business partner responsible for a recruitment process should be able to ask the respective hiring manager what stage the process is up to. The same hiring manager should be able to articulate the recruitment process. If the hiring manager is not clear on the process, or the stage they are up to, how could you expect a candidate to understand?

It is time to rethink the interview!

Through years of working with neurodivergent people and employers I am convinced that traditional interviews routinely screen out neurodivergent candidates. I have known dozens of neurodivergent candidates who have frozen during an interview, failed to mention core skills that were critical to the role, or presented as disinterested in the role. Interviews can be a poor predicator of a candidate's suitability to a role. Hundreds of studies reveal the profound limitations of the traditional interview. Interviews favour candidates who are attractive, sociable, articulate, and tall. They also favour manipulative candidates, or ones who know how to make a positive impression even in a brief interview. But those aren't always the best job performers (Moore, 2012).

Research from Davies et al. (2023) included participant interviews which highlight the challenges autistic and neurodivergent applicants face. Neurodivergent candidates felt that interviews focus on social skills and the ability to sell yourself, which put them at a disadvantage. Finally, this pointed suggestion, "Questions should be to the point – none of this reading between the lines malarky" (Davies et al., 2023, p. 1756).

Many recruiters and hiring managers use a phone screen in the recruitment process. You may have experienced this yourself when applying for a role. There are several ways recruiters can reduce anxiety for neurodivergent applicants while providing an opportunity to assess whether the candidate should progress to interview. These ways include:

- Provide advance notice of the call, avoid phoning unannounced;
- Try sending an SMS prior to explain the reason for the call and set a time;
- Be clear about what you want to discuss. If your aim is to screen applicants out and catch them off guard with an unexpected call, you will likely succeed; and
- Follow up the call with a written summary of the steps in the recruitment process.

Interview guide

Tips for interviewer:

- If in person, ensure the interview is conducted in a quiet location.
- Seat the candidate facing the wall, not looking out, to avoid distractions.
- Consider sitting adjacent to the candidate rather than across the table.
- Limit the panel to two persons, ideally the hiring manager and an HR or talent representative.
- Provide the interview questions 24 hours in advance of the interview.

Interview questions:

1. Start by introducing yourself, any colleagues, and the role. Also clearly explain the purpose of the interview. Ask the candidate if they have any questions.
2. Begin by explaining what the role does.
3. Why is this role of interest to you?
4. Do you have any special interests or hobbies?
5. Have you learnt anything new in the last 12 months? If yes, what motivated you to learn that?
6. Can you tell me a little bit about your <last role> or <field of study>.
7. Do you have a preference about where you work? Office, at home, a mixture? What about when you work, do you get more done in the evening, for example?

8. What expectations do you have for <insert employer's name>?

9. Do you have any questions for me?

Imagine you received a written application from a candidate who disclosed they are non-verbal in most situations. This was the scenario I first encountered in 2020. Even as an organisation dedicated to overcoming barriers to employment for neurodivergent people, this seemed like a bridge too far. What I hadn't anticipated was an employer who was open to an alternative recruitment process. Phone screens and voice interviews were replaced with a work sample and a virtual meeting with a difference. I wrote a blog about the alternative process, first published on the Xceptional website and later picked up by local print media, detailed below.

How to land your first job without saying a word

Aiden is an avid video gamer who dabbles in game development and programming. He once dreamed of making games and desktop apps for a living. However, as a non-verbal autistic teenager, living in the Blue Mountains, he rated his job prospects "somewhat low". He was worried that his social anxiety would prevent him from ever getting a job.

"I found that people didn't understand or appreciate me, especially at school in a mainstream environment", he says. His mother, Juliet, says that she found it challenging

to travel and organise activities that would allow Aiden "a bigger insight into the world". "[We] still have to deal with sensory issues and anxiety and try to find solutions in difficult situations. It can be very stressful and it involves the whole family", she says.

In March 2019, Juliet contacted Xceptional to find a work experience placement for Aiden's ICT TAFE course. Several months later Aiden attended an Xceptional workshop in Sydney that involved technical assessments and desktop games in a group environment to identify problem-solving, attention to detail, and reasoning skills. This process uncovered his unique aptitude in several fields.

Aiden was then invited to apply for a spatial data analytical software developer role with GeoSynergy, a Brisbane-based software company that provides consultancy and product development in the resources and utilities industries. Aiden had to complete four technical challenges to be considered for the job. "For the challenges, I had to program software to manipulate and/or visualise the data provided, and produce a result similar to what is described in the challenge description."

Geoff Osborn, Director of GeoSynergy, found that Aiden stood out in a field of 30 applicants for the role. "Aiden's responses were strong, quick and made intuitive sense to me." Without meeting face-to-face or exchanging any words, Geoff offered Aiden the job on a part-time basis. Aiden remembers feeling "impressed, a bit excited, nervous and anxious" when he received the job offer. He started work in January. Aiden works remotely in the comfort of his bedroom. His day-to-day tasks include creating prototypes for new software and creating diagrams or apps. "I enjoy working from home as I am relaxed in my own environment and I don't have the stress of being around lots of people and catching public transport", says Aiden. "The school has helped to negotiate my attendance so I can work two days a week and complete school on the other three days."

Aiden credits his strengths for thriving at GeoSynergy, such as learning new skills quickly from existing examples, solving problems through mental visualisation, and quick pattern recognition. "Also, prior knowledge has helped a lot. It has helped me to obtain new skills based on the software they are using and quickly creating solutions for the tasks." Aiden communicates at work through text messaging, emails, and diagrams. Everyone has been welcoming and supportive of his presence at work and his method of communication.

"I use [diagrams] to describe networks and the structure/ flow of the software when I find it hard to describe using words", he says. Aiden says he receives support from a job coach on learning to communicate and collaborate with co-workers to complete tasks. In addition, he has learned how to negotiate with his employer about his workload and hours for his upcoming HSC exams.

Geoff helps him with prioritising tasks and coordinating the task schedule. Two other colleagues help him on deploying software or programming in SQL."I feel happy that people

*understand who I am and what my strengths are at work",
says Aiden. "I am less worried about school, as I only attend
three days a week and that allows me to have less stress/
anxiety related to the school environment."*

*"I've realised I have the skills and ability to pursue a career
with my current knowledge which has given me confidence
and reduced my anxiety."* Aiden's mother, Juliet, says that
Aiden has been much happier since he started working
for GeoSynergy. *"I have to keep an eye that he has balance
and he's not too stressed out",* she says. *"I have negotiated
and had meetings with his high school teachers and TAFE
teachers to organise a way for Aiden to complete his HSC
while working with GeoSynergy."* Juliet says that Aiden
would find happiness as long as he was able to channel
his talent in work. *"We are living today with much more
education and awareness of people on the autism spectrum
and many employers are aware of the gifts and benefits of
employing such people. It makes me very happy."*

Aiden's manager, Geoff, praises Aiden's attention to detail
and efficiency working at GeoSynergy, as well as his *"strong
and diverse skill set"* across areas like problem-solving,
software development, and game engines. *"Teaching
Aiden how to effectively communicate via ticketing and
Skype has been my focus; however, this is the same for all
new staff",* says Geoff.

*"The process of writing out tickets and Skype messaging
lends itself to iteratively structuring questions and solutions,
so often I think it is as effective as voice or face-to-face*

communication." GeoSynergy has a remote team of workers scattered across Australia and overseas. According to Geoff, this workforce structure means that challenges such as social difficulties or sensitivities to noisy environments don't occur at all or are not relevant. "The advantages of being able to understand and solve complex problems, their work ethic, reliability ... are all upsides that far outweigh the downsides", says Geoff. "If you can't contribute to cracking an analytical problem or restating it, it doesn't really matter how social you are."

Aiden sees his current work becoming a full-time career one day. So, what is his advice for other autistic people like him to find the work they love to do? "Continue to build your knowledge around your special interests, think about and research what would be useful in the future (20+ years) as things are constantly changing and what is being used now could obsolete in a few years."

(Mercer, 2020)

A summary of neuroinclusive leaders' interview processes

Neuroinclusive leaders adapt the interview process to screen in a wider pool of candidates. The summary provided in Table 2 below has been taken from the Autism@Work Playbook, Annabi et al. (2021). It is worth considering what principles can be adopted for other neurotypes, and how smaller employers can adopt. I noted the shortened length of interviews and the opportunities for candidates to demonstrate their skills.

Table 2. Summary of interview processes

Who is involved?	Microsoft	SAP	EY	JPMorgan Chase
	Hiring managers	• Hiring managers	• A@W hiring managers	• Vendors
	• Hiring teams	• Hiring teams	• Job coaches	• HR recruiters
	• Job coaches	• Job coaches	• Business unit leaders	• Job coaches
	• A@W team	• AaW team	• A@W current employees/ self-advocates	• Hiring managers
	• A@W current employees/ self-advocates	• AaW current employees/ self-advocates	• HR	• Job coaches

	Microsoft	SAP	EY	JPMorgan Chase
How is screening conducted?	• Phone interview • Technical skills assessment	Qualifying interview (phone, virtual, or in-person)	Qualifying interview (phone or video) • Technical skills assessment (assessed by current A@W self-advocates)	Phone, in-person meet & greets • Intro to JPMC vendor and A@W process
What is the interview process like?	Multi-day in-person or virtual • 3 interviews kept to 50 minutes	• Candidate session (varies by location) • Screening call • Interviews • Technical assessment/demo (according to role)	One week virtual technical exercise and information exchange • One week in-person training • 45–60 minutes	Length of training depends on job function, typically 1–7 weeks (largely done by vendors) • Day of interviews: each component broken into 20–30 minutes & built-in breaks

	Microsoft	SAP	EY	JPMorgan Chase
What types of activities take place during the interview process?	Mock interviews Interview preparation/skill building • Technical assessments • Soft-skills exercises (especially collaboration activities) • Learning about MSFT	Soft skills exercises • Networking opportunities • Resume, portfolio, interview tips • Learning about SAP	Technical assessments and training (data analytics, economics, databases, Python, SQL) • Soft-skills (team-building communication exercises, team-based work simulations) • Learning about EY	Technical component if necessary (may include a test) • Learning about JPMC

	Microsoft	SAP	EY	JPMorgan Chase
What types of activities take place during the interview process?	Job coaches attend interview week to support candidates • Customised accommodations to meet candidate need • Built-in breaks and additional time between interviews • Catering to communication styles (option to communicate verbally or through text feature, written instructions and checklists provided in advance	Customised accommodations according to candidates' needs. Accommodations may include: • Sensory break during interview • Interviewer info provided to candidates in advance • Interview questions or topic lists provided in advance to candidates	Job coaches attend interview week with candidates • Customised accommodations for candidate need • Building in unstructured time during week	Customised accommodations for candidates • Building in unstructured time during week • Catering to communication styles • No open-ended questions • Focus on what candidates have accomplished, not what they want to do in the future

	Microsoft	SAP	EY	JPMorgan Chase
	• Training on neurodiversity for interviewers	• Interview prep session • Interview facilitator Interview best practices: • No rapid-fire questions, no surprise questions • Direct, focused questions • Manager enablement • Recruiter enablement		

Meeting the CEO of a large recruitment firm gave me a glimpse of the opportunities and the challenges of inclusive hiring where firms adopt a one-size-fits-all approach.

View from the 28th floor

The first thing that stuck me was the view. The 28th floor is perched above the Sydney Opera House, overlooking the world-famous harbour. The next thing I was greeted by was a beaming smile and crushing handshake. I later discovered that my diminutive colleague didn't receive the same handshake treatment!

Graeme is the MD of the Asia Pacific arm of a global talent firm. By any measure the firm is a success, responsible for 40,000 placements a year across Australia and New Zealand. The firm's clients include Federal and State Government and corporate giants. Their services range from graduate programmes to executive and board search and placement.

Graeme listens intently as we cover the barriers autistic and neurodivergent people face in finding and keeping a job. Their untapped skills and case studies of success. Despite his position and responsibility, Graeme is generous with his time. He was one of those people who make you feel like you are the only ones in the room, we had his full attention.

At the end of the presentation Graeme's beaming smile had faded, along with the morning sun. He looks up and confesses that "the recruitment process hasn't changed in 50 years. My dad went through the same process to get a job as I did, CV's and interviews". Graeme asks a question that seems simple, "what can we do? It sounds like we are overlooking some people we shouldn't be". In the remaining minutes of the meeting, I scramble though ideas of what the firm could do. The first thing out of my mouth was "give them a chance to show you what they can do". We then touch on lessons from neuroinclusion leaders, the value of education, and the limitations of a one-size-fits-all recruitment process.

On the street outside the soaring office building, I realised I had missed an opportunity. I had just spent 45 minutes with one of the region's most influential talent leaders. We had covered all the basics. But when speaking about neurodivergent talent the focus was "out there" – who can be brought into the firms, industrial recruitment process. What I had failed to point out in the moment was the firm who employ several thousand staff already have neurodivergent workers. When considering what changes could be made to better attract and retain neurodivergent talent, why not start by listening to the staff you already have?

I have been fortunate to work alongside several inclusive leaders who are taking concrete steps to attract, retain, and advance neurodivergent talent. As you will discover, inclusive leaders often face challenges in scaling hiring programmes due to internal bias and fears from managers.

Dirk's mission

Dirk is professional and polite, like most working in the public sector, but I can tell he is weary. For the past eight years Dirk has laboured to convince his public sector colleagues to follow his lead. Dirk is the executive sponsor for an employment programme which offers paid work experience, mentorship, and jobs for neurodivergent people. The programme started in the Education Department and has moved to Transport, Treasury, and Customer Service. Despite this success and the 80 neurodivergent people who have kickstarted their careers, Dirk wants to see more and is somewhat critical of the programme's success.

"Most managers I speak with want to have an impact, when I understand their reason to act it's a charitable, not a business, motivation", Dirk told me. He went on to say when the programme was first announced he was stunned by the response. Originally from Belgium, Dirk moved to Australia first to study, settling after graduation to begin a career in the public sector. Dirk knew of several hiring programmes in Europe and thought at a time of skills shortages the same could be replicated in Australia. "My colleagues and many from other departments were worried about how autistic people would fit in. Some thought that all autistic people were nonverbal, which did surprise me."

With quiet determination, patience, and precision, Dirk set about establishing the first employment programme for neurodivergent people in the state government's 174-year history. To design the programme, Dirk worked with a small team of HR business partners, neurodivergent staff, and a local non-profit. Time was invested to learn from the practices of global employment programmes such as those from EY, JPMorgan Chase, Microsoft, and SAP.

At the time of the programme launch, Dirk had convinced five hiring managers to take on an autistic worker, initially for a paid work trial of four weeks, then if successful for a 12-month contract. Dirk explained, "What struck me as odd from the hesitation was the managers, who already had neurodivergent staff – several of the team in records management were either ADHD or autistic." My hypothesis is the added pressure of a "programme" and senior leaders' attention added to the caution of hiring managers. Despite these concerns the pilot programme was a success, with all five participants completing the paid four-week trial and going onto a 12-month contract and then full-time employment. At the time of speaking with Dirk, three of the five are still employed by the department, several years later.

Dirk attributes the programme's success to the gateway strategy of offering paid work experience, which allowed candidates to demonstrate their skills in a real work context, rather than a formal interview. This, coupled with careful selection of the business functions and managers who have the right reason to act, recognising the business benefit over the charitable act. Dirk commented, "Roles in records management require a high attention to detail, and neurodivergent people can have an advantage for the business."

What weighs on Dirk is the lack of departments who have taken the lessons from the programme for everyday hiring. His team have published guides on interviewing, established an employer network, and offered free training on how to attract neurodivergent workers. In addition, the programme has faced some criticism from established neurodivergent employees, who question the coaching support and workplace adjustments programme staff receive. At the time of writing, Dirk is advising several departments on support for the neurodivergent staff already employed.

Programmes like Dirk's in the public sector and those from global giants like Microsoft's Neurodiversity Hiring Program and EY's Neurodiverse Centers of Excellence (NCoE) provide a welcome opportunity for some neurodivergent people to kickstart their careers. However, the programmes can be narrowly focused on white-collar jobs such as those in technology, costly to operate and simply out of reach for many employers. There are, however, several principles and practices that can be replicated at a smaller scale which we will explore in the coming chapters.

A fair go

Australian culture can be elusive to define. It combines over 40,000 years of First Nations history with 235 years of European settlement and waves of immigration from all corners of the globe. Indeed, Australia is a nation of immigrants, not always harmonious but a multicultural society which, like many developed nations, wrestles to define what it means to be Australian. One common phrase that cuts across diverse cultures in twenty-first-century Australia is the idea of a "fair go". The notion that everyone deserves a chance in life, where hard work, honesty, and grit count more than status, background, and heritage. It the part of Australian identity that I hold most dear.

Employers make hiring and promotion decisions every day. If you are reading this book, chances are you will at some stage have to decide on which individual receives an employment offer, and who gets promoted. If the concept of the fair go was applied to hiring and promotion decisions, then employers would strive to make choices based on meritocracy. This is the notion that employees are selected based on their skills, talent, and ability and that every candidate is judged solely on their fit for the job (Bika, 2022). Critically, a decision based on meritocracy is independent of other variables such as age, gender, socio-economic status, nationality, or disability.

However, human decisions are seldom based solely on rational facts. Instead of hiring and promotion decisions on meritocracy, a cocktail of biases including unconscious bias, affinity bias, and familiarity bias often lead to "mirrortocracy", where candidates are sought out who mirror current employees (LSE, 2022). Many employers list vague and hard to quantify skills such as "skilled leader", "creative thinker", or "team player" when advertising a job. Meritocratic decision-making is even less likely for positions where the required skills are difficult to measure and subject to individual interpretation (Castilla and Ranganathan, 2020).

We are all drawn to people like us; it is part of the human condition. To support employers in making merit-based decisions we must first understand the invisible barriers are inside our own minds. The University of California (2024) provides a helpful definition. "Bias is a prejudice in favour of or against one thing, person, or group compared with another usually in a way that's considered to be unfair. Biases may be held by an individual, group, or institution and can have negative or positive consequences."

Biases in recruitment

There are different types of biases:

1.   Conscious bias (also known as explicit bias); and
2.   Unconscious bias (also known as implicit bias).

Unconscious biases are social stereotypes about certain groups of people that individuals form outside their own conscious awareness. Everyone holds unconscious beliefs about various social and identity groups, and these biases stem from one's tendency to organise social worlds by categorising (University of California, 2024).

None of us have control over unconscious bias and beliefs. As Zhu (2023) explains, they are automatically triggered, and operate outside of our conscious awareness, influencing how we make daily decisions. Further, Carnahan and Moore (2023) note that affinity bias leads people to gravitate towards people who look, speak, and act like they do. This can lead to a preference for candidates similar to the manager and maybe justified as cultural fit (Carnahan and Moore, 2023).

Overall, employers I have met with look for candidates who are most like existing staff, whether they admit that or not. In cases where diverse candidates appear, communicate, or act differently, is it any wonder they can be overlooked in favour of those that fit the mould?

Is culture fit the enemy of diversity and inclusion?

Hiring decisions based on likeness to existing staff build homogenous teams. While often easier, it can lead to challenges, including:

- Blind spots, where information/knowledge is lacking due to a similarity of experience and perspectives;

- Groupthink, when homogenous teams favour consensus thinking, leading them to overlook negative consequence; and
- Poor decision-making that could affect the business's bottom line.

In contrast to culture fit, the concept of culture add is gaining traction. Trivella (2023) explains that companies who hire with culture in mind bring in people who see the world differently and have different perspectives.

Now that we are aware of the ways our minds work against making hiring and promotion decisions on meritocracy, we turn our attention to teachers of neurodivergent inclusion. First, the employers leading the way. Then, the best teachers of all, your own neurodivergent staff.

Conclusion

Throughout this chapter we have examined the hidden biases and barriers in our own minds, best practice from neuroinclusion leaders such as Microsoft and EY, as well as practical strategies to attract and recruit diverse candidates. I encourage anyone contemplating hiring to pause and ask yourself the question, who could you be missing out on? Critically evaluate your current process, and where possible engage your own neurodivergent staff, employee resource groups, or external experts to help answer the following questions:

- Is your recruitment process clearly communicated?
- Do your job descriptions clearly outline the core skills required?

- Could you provide all applicants an early win in the recruitment process?
- Are you providing an opportunity for candidates to demonstrate their skills?
- Are reasonable adjustments offered as standard?

As we continue through the employee lifecycle, employers must pay equal attention to onboarding, retaining, and developing. Simply put, the job is not done when an employer attracts and offers a role to a neurodivergent individual. My wish is to see neurodivergent candidates hired, of course, but equally important, they need to stay and advance.

5
Onboard and develop

One common misconception I encounter is that the job of neu-roinclusion is complete when a new employee starts. Many employers I speak with prioritise getting neurodivergent people into jobs and pay less attention to onboarding and advance-ment. My hypothesis is that this is due to a dedicated pro-gramme – company-wide quotas are a part of a broader diversity and inclusion agenda. Let us consider that for every known neurodivergent staff member there are many more already employed. Depending on the size of the organisation, this could be a significant number. Beyond your staff, there are of course neurodivergent customers, shareholders, neighbours, and so on.

As we continue to explore neuroinclusion through the employee lifecycle, it's time to consider what interventions can improve the onboarding experience and contribute to retention and advancement. This chapter will draw again on the stages of the employee lifecycle. We will cover stages 3. Onboard and 4. Develop as outlined below.

1. Attract: A potential applicant learns of the organisation and forms opinions about whether they would be interested in working there.

2. Recruit: Candidates move through the search and hiring process, including job ads, CV screening, and interviews.

3. **Onboard: New employees are brought into the organisation and trained.**

4. **Develop: Employees enhance their skills and advance their careers within the organisation through additional learning and development.**

5. Retain: Employees are encouraged to remain in the organisation through various organisational practices, such as offering benefits, additional training and promotion.

6. Separate: Employees either move to another organisation or retire and are offboarded.

(Cattermole, 2019)

Throughout this chapter we will cover:

- The value of training for employers;
- Unpacking reasonable adjustments;
- The importance of understanding your people;
- Practical onboarding considerations for neurodivergent staff; and
- Inclusion hacks for ADHD, autistic, and dyslexic staff.

In 2017, the *Guardian* newspaper published an anonymous letter from an autistic employee as a part of a series, "What I wish I could tell my boss" (Anonymous, 2017). While reading this chapter, consider the content of this letter and its onboarding implications.

"My autism is not a problem"

"I need you to understand that while my condition may seem crippling to you, I actually have a pretty good life.

When you offered me the job, it seemed perfect. You said I blew the competition away and you wanted me to start as soon as possible. You beat my current pay and promised a family-style atmosphere where emphasis was on the 'right personality'.

As someone with autism, I wasn't looking for special treatment. If anything, telling you about my condition has made my job worse. Now rather than being seen as 'cutely eccentric' I am 'the one with the developmental disability'.

I didn't complain about the fluorescent lighting, or when you moved me from a quiet office to a busy one, or when you cancel our meetings and then lean in the doorway and regurgitate your weight-loss goals to me.

If I mention that these things make me panic, want to vomit, make my ears ring – you tell me to get it together. Then you ask me for my personal input on autistic patients.

I am not here to tick boxes on an equal opportunities form. When I told you I needed support in the workplace you immediately extended my probationary period, knowing that this new insecurity around job safety was directly related to a disability.

Yes, I can hear you whispering two offices away through closed doors. Just like I can hear washing machines three doors down on my road or my partner opening a plaster.

Yes, I know my eye contact is poor, but don't bully me into making it. And do not touch me. It makes my skin burn so I'd rather you didn't. Yes, I do have very rigid routines and travelling alone is difficult, but I manage.

I need you to understand that these things may seem crippling to you, but actually I have a pretty good life. A couple of good friends, partner, planned holiday, and a mix of interests.

I wish I could tell you this is the first job where I have felt disabled. You remind me weekly of my special needs. That time you shouted at us in a meeting, I began shaking because the volume of your words made me feel sick. And afterwards everyone else was asked if they were OK, but I was avoided. You told people to leave me alone and whispered that I just couldn't cope.

I wish I could tell you how confused I was when you encouraged me to make a statement against a discriminatory member of staff and said you'd back me. When your boss was there and told me I shouldn't be pursuing it, you said nothing. Later, you told other staff that you thought I was trying to catch out the company for my own personal gain.

HR policies state I should take this up with your boss, but the one time I told them about it, I wasn't allowed back in the meeting.

When you say: 'Don't you worry that if you have kids they'll be autistic?' I need you to know that only you feel shame and worry about my disability. For me, my autism isn't a problem."

This harrowing account is by no means isolated. Over the course of the last eight years, I have listened to dozens of similar accounts. In Chapter 2 we heard about Brad's experience with manager Nate, which centred on communication styles and an inflexible, one-size-fits-all approach. The interventions that we will cover in this chapter have the dual purpose of preventing psychological injury and maximising the potential of neurodivergent staff. In addition, we will cover what employers can do to prepare managers and teams for incoming neurodivergent staff.

Onboarding. The first 90 days

Through years of working with employers to attract neurodivergent talent, I have been asked to compromise on many services. "Do we really need job coaching?", for example. I'm not proud to admit that sometimes compromises have been made. However, the one element of the recruitment and onboarding process I have not been willing to compromise on is neuroinclusive training.

The value of neuroinclusion training

Even though the employers I have worked with already have neurodivergent staff, it is often the first time they are knowingly onboarding an autistic, ADHD, or dyslexic employee. Smith and Kirby (2021, p. 189) argued "appropriate and targeted training is often the key to improving communications, addressing misconceptions and building a positive environment before or during induction".

When considering training neurodiversity autism at work, effective training is best performed by those with deep knowledge of neurodivergence, ideally by those with lived experience. In recent years, I have worked with employers to co-design training by engaging with HR business partners and employee resource groups. Many neurodiversity experts such as auticon, asa, and Uptimize offer workshop style and on-demand training for small to medium enterprise employers. Depending on your region, many non-profits and community organisations offer training.

Whoever you select to partner with in delivering neuroinclusion training, what you cover is as important as who presents the information. The following outlines the core curriculum from asa, which is offered as a guide:

- Definitions and neurodivergent variances (e.g. autism, ADHD, dyslexia);
- Exploration of neurodivergent experiences in the workplace;
- How neurodivergence can present at work; and
- How a neuroinclusive work environment helps everyone.

Understanding disclosure and reasonable adjustments

Disclosure is a key step to obtaining reasonable adjustments in the workplace. Neurodivergent employees and those with varied disabilities are protected by legislation in many countries, mandating reasonable workplace adjustments to ensure inclusivity and equal opportunities. Protective legislation includes: The Americans with Disabilities Act (ADA.gov, 2024); the UK's Equality

Act 2010 (gov.uk, 2024); and Australia's Disability Discrimination Act 1992 (Federal Register of Legislation, 2023).

In many cases the reasonable adjustments neurodivergent people need are neither complex or costly; however, some employers have shared concerns about adjustments and opening themselves up to requests from existing staff.

Before continuing, it is worth acknowledging the concepts of equality and equity. Two words that sound very similar, however, are vastly different. According to George Washington University (2020), "Equality means each individual or group of people is given the same resources or opportunities. Equity recognises that each person has different circumstances and allocates the exact resources and opportunities needed to reach an equal outcome". Applying the concept of equity to neuroinclusion, Zindell (2024) concluded that neurodivergent employees require specific support in the workplace. The most commonly requested supports, in order of importance were:

- Regular check ins;
- Flexible work hours;
- Quiet workplaces;
- Mentorship programmes; and
- Customised training.

Having observed these adjustments in action I can concur that they can make a significant difference. Regular check ins can support staff like Amy, who despite her skills often second guesses herself, so regular check ins can ensure she stays on track. For some colleagues with sleep disturbances, flexible work hours mean the difference between performing or just surviving. For me personally, quiet workplaces are not just a "nice to have". I simply can't function without them.

Unfortunately, there is evidence to suggest that granting reasonable adjustments can have a negative effect due to ableist responses from staff without disability. Some existing staff can object to adjustments, with accommodations for invisible disabilities viewed as less deserving (Snyder et al., 2010 in Mellifont, 2021). Fevre et al. (2013) stated "co-workers may ill-treat employees with disabilities because of what they believe to be unreasonable or unfair variations in workplace norms for such employees" (Mellifont, 2021, p. 302). Managers and HR business partners need to be alert to any negative sentiment and provide education and coaching to address such bias.

The following scenario is an amusing example of an employer making assumptions about the needs of neurodivergent staff.

Understanding your people

Audrey was five months into her new role as Head of Finance for a national charity. While Audrey's colleagues were welcoming and the workload reasonable, she found the office setting weird. For starters, most of the office lights were off during the day. Natural light and desk lamps were a poor substitute for overhead lighting. The office was also incredibly quiet; you could hear yourself breathing. If there was a ever phone call outside Audrey's office, she simply shut the door and continued working under dim lights. The last Friday of each month, the office got together for a wrap up that included birthday cake for anyone celebrating that month. At this month's gathering, Audrey got chatting with the Head of Marketing. She asked the question that had been plaguing her for months, why do you work in the dark? It is like a morgue in here. Gavin's response shocked Audrey, "the lighting is for you, same as the lack of noise or music. We used to play music in the office. Knowing you were coming, HR suggested we cut the lights and stop playing music." Audrey had been open about her autism and sensory needs when applying for the role. However, she never asked or was offered specific adjustments relating to lighting or sound. It was assumed that these changes would be appreciated. They not only surprised and mildly frustrated Audrey, but also alienated some of her colleagues.

Several months later, the office is once again adequately lit and music is enjoyed by all. When Audrey needs to concentrate on deep work, she either shuts the office door or puts on headphones, with – wait for it – music.

We can all make assumptions about what others might need. In Audrey's case, a simple checklist of what adjustments she needed would have made all the difference. Marilyn, a neurodivergent Human Resource leader for a global pharmaceutical company, has developed what she calls a standard operating procedure for people. Marilyn explained that every machine or process the company uses has a standard operating procedure, which they refer to as a SOP. To Marilyn's surprise, when she was onboarded into her role there was not a SOP for people, something she has now addressed and made available throughout the organisation.

Outlined below is an example of an onboarding and development checklist that I have adapted from several industry examples including Xceptional and auticon. The checklist (see Table 3) is designed to support a tailored onboarding and development plan for neurodivergent staff. As has been suggested to me several times, it is worth considering adopting this approach for all new employees.

Table 3. Onboarding and development checklist

Which of the following adjustments are essential for your job?
❑ Noise-cancelling headphones
❑ Flexible hours and start times
❑ The ability to work from home at least two days per week
❑ The ability to work remotely more than two days a week
❑ Are there any other adjustments that will support you?
Communication and learning preferences
❑ Written communication with detailed instructions
❑ Clear agendas for meetings
❑ Face-to-face, in-person or walking meetings
❑ The opportunity to learn by task demonstration
❑ The opportunity to learn by doing
❑ A learning plan with clear expectations and milestones
❑ A proxy to present work or information to large groups on my behalf
Social
❑ Limited social interactions preferably with individuals or small groups only
❑ The option to not attend large gatherings (either social or business)
❑ The opportunity to organise team gatherings and activities

Sensory
❑ The opportunity to work in a quiet environment
❑ A workspace with no or minimal surrounding distractions
❑ The ability to work at the end of a desk, away from high-traffic areas

Management
❑ Regular communication and feedback from my manager
❑ Unambiguous feedback from my manager that is detailed and direct
❑ The opportunity to ask questions and clarify instructions

When introducing neurodivergent staff the following disclosure consent checklist can be helpful:

- I consent to Human Resources and my manager being informed that I identify as neurodivergent in order to facilitate workplace support.
- I consent to my immediate team members being informed that I identify as neurodivergent in order to facilitate workplace support.
- I consent to colleagues outside of my immediate team being informed that I identify as neurodivergent in order to facilitate workplace support.

Onboarding email template

The following onboarding email can be adapted as needed to introduce a neurodivergent individual once consent is obtained. Consider ways you could inclusively and respectively co-design your own version with existing neurodivergent staff.

Subject: Welcoming Our Newest Team Member [Employee's Name]

I'm thrilled to introduce our newest team member, [employee's name], who brings a wealth of talent and unique perspectives to our [team/department]. They have a background in [add professional history] and [add personal interest or anecdote]. [Employee's name] has chosen to share that they identify as neurodivergent, a term that encompasses a range of neurological differences such as autism, ADHD, and dyslexia. We are committed to fostering an inclusive and supportive work environment for all our team members, and I encourage each of you to join me in extending a warm welcome to [employee's name].

To ensure a smooth transition and create a workplace that accommodates everyone's needs, we'd like to ask for your cooperation in understanding and supporting [employee's name]. Here are a few tips to keep in mind:

1. Be Open and Approachable: If [employee's name] chooses to share more about their neurodivergent identity, listen attentively, and be open to learning from their unique perspectives. Remember, everyone is on a different stage of their identity journey.

2. Ask the Person: If you have questions about preferences or working styles, ask [employee's name]. Asking questions shows you are accommodating, supportive, and collaborative. Note that the way questions are asked, for example, over the phone, email, or in person, may influence the results. Whenever possible, first ask for the individual's preferred communication method.

3. Focus on Strengths: Consider the strengths and talents [employee's name] brings to our team. Embrace a strengths-based approach, acknowledging the valuable contributions they can make.

If you have questions or would like more information about how to support [employee's name], feel free to reach out to [manager's name] or our Human Resources department.

Let's all work together to make [employee's name]'s onboarding experience positive and welcoming.

Thank you for your cooperation, and let's look forward to creating a supportive and inclusive environment for everyone on the team.

To follow are three scenarios that collectively highlight the importance of having effective on-boarding processes and procedures in place for neurodivergent employees.

Understanding work preferences and behaviours

"Hi, I'm Autumn and I may interrupt you." This is how Autumn introduces herself when meeting new colleagues. Given the frequency she changes assignments, it's an introduction that has been well tested. Autumn's latest project is as a senior data analyst for a transport firm. Autumn prefers the flexibility of contracting projects which are typically 6 to 12 months in length. In addition to her data analysis skills, Autumn has a deep interest in design and psychology. After confirming the time for a conversation, I had the chance to speak with Autumn about her experience in the workplace

and her perspective as a late diagnosed autistic and ADHD woman. I was not expecting Autumn's advice on starting a new role to be things which anyone can adopt.

Growing up, Autumn knew she was bright but different. Struggling with social conversations and being sensitive to crowds and noise, she compiled a toolkit of learned behaviours to cope. As a keen observer of people, Autumn would look for the best communicator in a group based on how others reacted, and then mirror them. When we speak Autumn points out that she is deliberate about her cadence of speech and has to remember to pause after making a point. "Language is not my language", Autumn shares. I love this quote and promise it will go into the book. Our collective ADHD means we frequently interrupt each other, but the conversation flows in its own way. Autumn has a gift for numbers and the analysis of data; she can see connections between datasets that others miss. Unlike many neurodivergent women I have spoken with, Autumn seems comfortable with her skills and success.

Autumn has been fortunate to work for inclusive employers like Atlassian, along with others she won't name but have clearly been regrettable. Through her career, Autumn has kept her dual diagnosis largely private. Instead, she greets new colleagues with behaviours they may expect. From interrupting colleagues to coming across as blunt, Autumn focuses on her behaviours, not her conditions. Her perspective is that diagnosis is shared on a need-to-know basis. On the rare occasions when Autumn has disclosed in the workplace, she has experienced a range of reactions, some supportive, others condescending. Autumn recalls one manager started speaking slowly, as if English was her second language!

When onboarding and developing new employees, Autumn suggests education is critical. Autumn feels that stigma of any difference or perceived weakness needs to be addressed. Most managers Autumn has known have a limited understanding of neurodivergence and tend to avoid the discussion out of fear of doing or saying the wrong thing. Autumn does empathise; it is part of the human condition to be fearful of anyone who is different. She suggests she is xenopobic, preferring a community of like-minded people, many of whom are same sex attracted and neurodivergent. "I prefer to work and play with people like me, so why wouldn't managers?", Autumn admits.

Autumn's advice for hiring managers is to get past the stereotypes and learn about neurotypes and how they present in men, women and non-binary individuals. She would also love to see neurodivergent leaders share their diagnosis as modelling from the top will normalise speaking about difference. In the meantime Autumn will keep introducing herself by focusing on her behaviours rather than her neurotype.

The conversation with Autumn has inspired me to think about practical steps that employers can take to onboard and develop new staff. Think about the last time you started a new job – how were you introduced? If it was a casual or part-time job the introduction may have covered the basics, your name and what days you are available. For part-time, contract and full-time roles there may have been more detail on your background provided to your new colleagues, assuming the new hire has met with their manager.

What if instead of covering where a new hire has studied or worked previously, they were introduced with detail on how they work? Providing a personalised onboarding plan can make the difference in setting up new hires for success. Try combining the Onboarding Checklist in Table 3 with detail on how your new hire likes to give and receive feedback, as well as how their manager can best support them. Remember, if in doubt ask the person.

Practical considerations – my own experiences

It has been 20 years since I started my first professional job. I had moved with my wife to take a role in business development with a regional marketing and communications company. The Sunday before I started, I had practised driving to the office just to make sure I didn't get lost on the first day in a new city.

Arriving on day one – early, of course – I was underwhelmed by how prepared my new employer was. While my new manager and team knew of my pending arrival, there were several gaps in my onboarding. For starters, I didn't have a desk or laptop to start work. I fumbled through the first few days by meeting new colleagues and filling out paper onboarding forms. All staff in our division were to begin reading a professional development book that Monday; it may sound small, but there was no copy for me. It took a fortnight to gain access to all the IT systems which coincided with a new laptop and, yes, a desk. For someone who prefers structure and routine, this was a difficult start.

While this example may seem trivial, small details, if overlooked during onboarding, can make a big difference and threaten a new employee's development. This is particularly true for neuro-divergent staff who have difficulty navigating change.

Platform 12

Otis was late, which if you knew him was very unusual. Otis also looked worried and rushed, like it had been a stressful morning. The team had recently moved from a suburban to city office. Today was the first day in the new office. The operations team managing the move had planned this change for months. A dedicated project management office was established, IT contractors supported set up, and well-crafted communications regularly shared with staff and customers. The only thing Otis and the team needed to do was turn up at the new location on Monday.

Otis was a person who valued routine. He had come accus-tomed to the 412 bus route from their home to the subur-ban office. Preferring solitude to noise, Otis left home at 6.30 a.m. to ensure he had a quiet and comfortable commute to work. Otis was diagnosed with autism and anxiety in high school. Despite being intensely private, Otis is open to sharing that he struggles with crowds and finds changes to routine challenging to cope with.

On this particular Monday morning, Otis found himself at the bottom of platform 12 of Central Station, not knowing which way to turn. The station had been upgraded since he was last there. There were five potential exits, but none of them included the street the new office was located on. Otis finds it difficult to engage in conversation with strangers, so the thought of asking for directions was terrifying. Minutes went by, train after train arrived, and people hurried off to work, leaving the station through one of the five exits.

After what seemed like an hour and may have been as much as 30 minutes, a transport officer spotted Otis and approached to offer assistance. This simple act of taking the first step made the world of difference for Otis. He was able to explain where he needed to be and promptly ushered to exit 3. Finally, by the time Otis arrived at the new office, his morning was a wreck, and it took him several hours to regain composure.

Do know what would have made a difference for Otis, or any anyone else who was unfamiliar with the new location? A guide of how to get to the new location. The guide could have included public transport advice which detailed which exit to take, parking options if they are available, directions from the street. I have known employers take this to the next level, providing photos of the office and foyer and include links to Google Street View or Apple Maps.

Whether onboarding, managing change, or developing new staff, knowing your team and not assuming knowledge is advisable. The tips shared in this chapter may seem like stating the obvious. It could have seemed obvious that providing the address of the new office was enough; it clearly wasn't.

Below is a first-day checklist that can help neurodivergent employees to be welcomed and including in the workplace (see Table 4).

Table 4. First day checklist

Location
❏ Office location, public transport, parking options
❏ Pictures of the office building and foyer, if applicable
❏ Virtual access via <Zoom, Teams, Google Meet>
❏ Expectations about in person or virtual attendance
❏ If virtual, set expectations about camera on or off
Reporting and support
❏ Direct managers given name, preferred name, contact details
❏ Buddy or mentor given name, preferred name, contact details
❏ HR contact given name, preferred name, contact details
Dress code
❏ Business attire, e.g. suit pants and jacket with dress shoes
❏ Smart casual, e.g. pants, dress, or jeans and a shirt with dress shoes
❏ Casual, jeans, shirt, casual shoes, e.g. joggers.
Employee calendar
❏ Daily check ins at 9.30 a.m., via <Zoom, Teams, Google Meet>
❏ Wednesday meeting with manager, 10 a.m. in person
❏ Friday all company meeting, 10 a.m. via <Zoom, Teams, Google Meet>

Onboarding plan

❏ Detailed agenda on who to meet, when, and what will be discussed

❏ Timetable for the first two weeks

❏ OH&S induction

❏ HR induction

❏ IT systems induction and set up including hardware, software, security access

Employee development

Leading HR platform Culture Amp (2024) defined employee development as "the shared initiative of an employer and employee to strengthen the employee's skill sets and expand their knowledge." They suggest that effective development is ongoing and personalised, containing three elements:

1. **Experience:** On-the-job experiences that help employees grow (e.g. stretch tasks, special products, mentoring others, etc.);

2. **Exposure:** Learning through observation (e.g. working with a coach, seeking feedback, shadowing, networking, etc.); and

3. **Education:** Structured learning (e.g. courses, books, conferences).

Powell (2002) argued that most job-related learning is informal, unplanned, and happens while on the job. While organisational development tools like learning management systems have advanced since Powell's observations, there is room for improvement. As we have learnt, neurotypes each present with differences in learning styles. However, it is generally accepted that more structure rather than less and clear instructions will be beneficial to neurodivergent employees and managers. To make the most of the onboarding and development phases, create a personalised onboarding and development plan for any new staff.

While acknowledging that everyone is different, there are some adjustments that are useful to consider. The adjustments outlined below have been observed in my work with neurodivergent people and employers. It is worth remembering that, for recently diagnosed staff, these adjustments may be particularly helpful. In my experience many recently diagnosed individuals, particularly women, are unaware of their own needs with respect to adjustments. Further research is required to understand why this is the case. My observation is that masking behaviour has become entrenched and will need to be unlearned as an individual understands more about their neurodivergence and what workplace support they may need to thrive.

Inclusion hacks to support the development of autistic employees

- **Clear communication:** Provide explicit and clear communication for everything. Avoid common clichés and idioms like, "at the end of the day", "we need to switch on", "let's put our best foot forward", "we are going to circle back", "I've got to socialise this idea", and many more. These common sayings lack literal meaning and often confuse neurodivergent thinkers. Instructions for a task are most effective if written down.

- **Flexible work:** This is not a preference but a necessity for many neurodivergent people. Flexibility can include flexible schedules, remote work, or allowing for breaks to manage sensory overload or anxiety. These are essential to provide the mental space to maintain performance.

- **Time management:** Autistic staff appreciate consistency and routine. Where possible, provide at least 24 hours' notice for meetings or any changes to schedule.

- **Sensory considerations:** Pay attention to the physical environment. Question what can be done to minimise noise levels, soften fluorescent lighting, or identify designated quiet areas, if beneficial. Understand whether your autistic employee also has sensory sensitivities, such as sensory processing disorder. Provide noise-cancelling headphones if required.

- **Training and awareness:** Managers and staff can't contribute to an inclusive and productive culture for autistic people without an understanding and awareness of autism. Engage in open dialogue to understand autistic people's needs and work together to identify reasonable adjustments that will enable them to perform at their best.

- **Meeting hacks:** In team meetings once a month have the first five minutes of common banter via chat function. Always have a clear agenda which is provided the day before the meeting. Avoid putting autistic staff on the spot in a meeting, unless you have previously seen them respond in similar circumstances. Provide ample warning, "Sarah, I am going to ask you shortly for an update on your security project, but first let's cover finance."

- **Structured support:** Implement structured support systems such as mentorship programmes, buddy systems, or employee resource groups. Where possible, these initiatives should be led by autistic employees themselves.

For further suggestions visit www.neurodiversityhub.org/resources-for-employers

Inclusion hacks to support the development of ADHD employees

- **ADHD-friendly meetings:** Ensure face-to-face or virtual meetings are concise, providing clear agendas in advance. Consider shorter, focused sessions to accommodate attention spans. For longer meetings introduce a short movement break every 45 to 60 minutes.

- **Flexible work arrangements:** Where possible, offer flexibility in work hours and workspaces. Providing accommodations that cater to individual needs will enable staff to manage their energy levels effectively. For example, when in the office stagger start times and offer out-of-the-way, focused workspaces. Alternatively, encourage people to take calls outside, or while walking.

- **Sensory considerations:** Pay attention to the physical environment. Question what can be done to minimise noise levels and distractions. Provide noise-cancelling headphones if required.

- **Supportive systems:** Tools such as time management apps, for example, Screen Time on Apple, organisational software, or noise-cancelling headphones, to help individuals stay on task and minimise distractions.

- **Structured environment:** Encourage staff to establish structured routines, visual schedules, and task lists to enhance organisation and provide a sense of predictability.

- **Clear communication:** Provide clear instructions and expectations, encourage staff to break down complex tasks into manageable steps. Regular check ins and written communication can help reinforce understanding and minimise miscommunication.

- **Emotional and mental health support:** Offer resources for managing emotional and mental health

For further suggestions visit https://adhdlounge.com/creating-an-adhd-friendly-workplace-practical-tips-and-tools-for-employ ers/https://supernormal.com/blog/navigating-adhd-workplace

Inclusion hacks to support the development of dyslexic employees

- **Text accessibility:** Use dyslexia-friendly fonts like OpenDyslexic or Arial. Ensure documents have adequate white space, larger text sizes, and clear contrast between text and background. Provide written materials in multiple formats (audio, video, and text-to-speech tools).

- **Clear and concise communication:** Break down instructions into smaller, manageable steps. Avoid using complex language or jargon; use plain language and direct statements. Provide written summaries of verbal instructions and important points from meetings.

- **Structured and predictable environment:** Maintain a structured work environment with consistent routines and clear expectations. Provide checklists and templates for common tasks to help with organisation. Allow extra time for reading and writing tasks.

- **Assistive technology:** Encourage the use of assistive technologies such as speech-to-text software, digital note-taking tools, spelling and grammar check, and reading aids like coloured overlays or line trackers. Implement time-management apps. Suggested apps and software include:

  o   https://app.grammarly.com/

  o   https://opendyslexic.org/

  o   https://trello.com/

  o   https://monday.com/

  o   https://blocksite.co/

  o   https://rewordify.com/

Conclusion

Through this chapter, we have discussed strategies to support the effective onboarding and development of neurodivergent staff. From planning the first day and induction to the development of skills, adopting a personalised approach is recommended. Above all, don't assume all the neurodivergent staff you are welcoming can figure out what needs to be done and what the expectations are for themselves. Understanding your people and what they need to be successful is key. We will continue through the employee lifecycle in Chapter 6 where we detail neuroinclusion strategies for retention, advancement, and separation.

6

Retain, advance, and separate

As we continue to explore neuroinclusion through the employee lifecycle, we turn our attention to retaining neurodivergent employees and managing separation. Hence, we will cover stages 5 and 6 as highlighted below.

1. Attract: A potential applicant learns of the organisation and forms opinions about whether they would be interested in working there.
2. Recruit: Candidates move through the search and hiring process, including job ads, CV screening, and interviews.
3. Onboard: New employees are brought into the organisation and trained.
4. Develop: Employees enhance their skills and advance their careers within the organisation through additional learning and development.
5. **Retain and advance: Employees are encouraged to remain and advance in the organisation through various organisational practices, such as offering benefits, additional training, and promotion.**
6. **Separate: Employees either move to another organisation or retire and are offboarded.**

(Cattermole, 2019)

Throughout this chapter we will be covering the following topics:

- Why people leave jobs;
- Distortions to advancement;
- Retention strategies; and
- Constructive offboarding practices.

Retainment

Why people leave jobs

It's often said that "people don't quit a job, they quit a boss" (Goler et al., 2018). While employees may initially be attracted to a company's mission, values, and opportunities, their daily experiences and interactions with their managers significantly influence their decision to stay or leave.

As we seek to understand why people leave jobs, it is worth pausing to consider what employees really want from work. According to Popelka (2022) we've known for decades that good working conditions are necessary to retain and advance talent. These conditions include fair compensation, a safe and stable environment, and career growth. While such factors are sufficient to attract and retain talent in the current economy, they are not enough on their own.

Smart companies and great leaders need to fully engage and unleash people's potential. To do that, leaders must go beyond the basics of good working conditions to provide the following four pillar notions:

- **Purpose:** to find meaning in their work;

- **Agency:** to have some say over how, when, and where they work;
- **Belonging:** to feel part of a community, even if they are remote, freelance, or part-time; to be part of a diverse community; and
- **Recognition:** to be acknowledged for their contributions, in multiple forms, on a regular basis (Popelka, 2022).

Of course, pay is important, and as many countries grapple with cost-of-living pressures workers are seeking more money to keep pace with inflation. Your current or future neurodivergent employees are not immune from these pressures or the need for purpose, agency, belonging, and recognition. Neurodivergent employees may have specific needs, related to their neurotype. In Chapter 4, we learned that the most requested adjustments included regular check ins, flexible hours, and quiet workspaces (Zindell, 2024).

It stands to reason that employers who fail to provide these commonly requested adjustments are at risk of losing their neurodivergent staff. Goler et al. (2018) recognised the importance of managers in an employee's decision to leave but suggested that narrow, poorly designed, and unchallenging jobs were the main factor. Managers are responsible for assigning work that uses their team's skills and experience. Creating time and space to understand the skills, untapped potential, and motivation of each member of a team is not an easy task. Start by finding out what motivates each person, what they are learning or doing in their spare time, and why. Then, wherever possible, provide an opportunity to taste and see, sample different parts of the role as early as possible. This may involve rotating through different disciplines such as product design and customer service during an onboarding period.

Retention strategies

Mortensen and Edmonson (2023) argued that the key to retaining staff is "implementing an employee value proposition – a system composed of four interrelated factors":

1. **Material offerings** includes pay, office space, equipment, flexibility and benefits;

2. **Opportunities to develop and grow includes the ways employers** help employees acquire new skills. Examples include training and promotion;

3. **Connection and community** relate to the benefits that come from being a part of a large group. They include relationships, accountability, and feelings of belonging; and

4. **Meaning and purpose** are an organisation's reasons for existing which align with an employee's desire to contribute to a higher purpose, or mission.

Advancement

Neurodivergent people leaders bring a depth of lived and professional experience to their workplaces. In the scenario outlined below, the Chief People Officer of a global technology company offers insights into the advancement of neurodivergent staff that are delivering spectacular results.

> *Luke is a man who has found his place in life and feels settled in his position. As the Chief People Officer of a global technology company, it was my privilege to speak with Luke*

about his experiences. Identifying as neurodivergent, with a dual diagnosis of ADHD and dyslexia, Luke offers rich a personal and professional perspective.

Luke considers his career success to be a product of persistence, luck, and his ability to thrive during times of change when those around him flounder. Luke has held senior positions in Europe, the Middle East, and now Australia; he was awarded a PhD for his studies on organisational development, while working full time. The PhD, Luke says, was 9 years of work, 80,000 words. It was something he said yes to quickly and enjoyed for the first three months!

Having held senior positions early in his career allowed Luke to surround himself with people who have strengths in areas of his weakness. Luke freely admits to a lack of attention to detail and a propensity to rush ahead with decisions.

The range of issues Luke and his team are managing is mind bending. The company operates in 28 counties, with 7 languages, and 10,000 staff. The company has acquired several competitors in Luke's time, and each acquisition presents a new set of people challenges. In Luke's 5 years, the company has acquired 40 businesses around the world. Thankfully, Luke loves the dopamine hit of a new challenge.

Strong leadership and a result-driven, non-hierarchical culture has led to extraordinary success. The company is a global leader in its field, enjoying lower staff turnover and higher productivity than any rival. Luke attributes this to the unique way that talent is recognised, onboarded, and developed. The company has a healthy appreciation for the unique problem-solving ability and persistence which many neurodivergent individuals can offer.

What sets this company apart from others is the onboarding and rotation of new staff. Firstly, new staff are introduced to each other, their manager, buddy, and the first of three rotation teams. Luke shares that he has never felt more at ease being himself. The company attracts more than its share of unique characters. It values skills and persistence above all. Well-dressed, self-promoting graduates from prestigious schools need not apply!

Over the course of the next six months, new staff will rotate through three projects which are carefully chosen based on the needs of the company, the skills of each individual, and the range of products in development. At the end of the six months, new staff will have detailed knowledge of at least three products, and have worked with up to 50 colleagues. Through the process, a rotations manager and buddy regularly check in with new staff and track their progress though a productivity application.

Incredibly, at the end of the third rotation, each new staff member can choose their next assignment, which is typically 12 months in a product team. Imagine that, having the agency to choose which team! Of course, there is some give and take. For instance, 20 new staff can't pick the same product team. New staff are treated like the mature adults they are; often the new staff work out among themselves who goes where.

The rotation programme and freedom to choose assignments is particularly important for neurodivergent staff. Luke has noticed that even the most introverted staff finish their rotations with at least two strong connections and know many people across the organisation. The exposure to multiple product teams would act as a counter to staff who avoid social gatherings and networking. It would also support staff who are unlikely to put themselves forward for stretch assignments such as novel projects or additional responsibilities which are beyond their primary role.

All staff, regardless of background, appearance, or formal qualifications, are judged on their contribution and care is taken to ensure equal access to opportunity. At the time we spoke several neurodivergent staff were selected for a global leadership programme, the first step on the path to senior leadership.

My conclusion is the focus on skills over degrees, the rotation programme, clearly defined productivity goals, room for autonomy, and tailored support allowed these future leaders to show their potential.

The glass ceiling

In Chapter 4 we learnt that hiring decisions are seldom based purely on merit. Decisions on who to hire are influenced by a cocktail of biases, including unconscious bias, affinity bias, and familiarity bias (Carnahan and Moore, 2023; Zhu, 2023; Rivera, 2012). Biases also influence managers who make decisions on advancement. Once employed, research demonstrates that advancement is not even.

Employees from minority groups lag their colleagues in compensation and advancement. Have you heard of or experienced a glass ceiling? "The glass ceiling, a phrase first introduced in the 1980s, is a metaphor for the invisible and artificial barriers that block women and minorities from advancing up the corporate ladder to management and executive positions" (Johns, 2013, p. 1).

Distortions to advancement

While the glass ceiling is a useful metaphor for uneven access to promotion, it does not explain why this inequity exists for many neurodivergent employees. In the next section, I will briefly cover some of the research on the distortions to such advancement in the workplace and then suggest tactics that inclusive leaders can deploy to address these challenges.

Stereotypes

In the 2009 film *Up in the Air*, George Clooney's character Ryan Bingham quips, "I'm like my mother, I stereotype. It's faster" (IMDb, 2024).

Like it or not, we all stereotype, either consciously or unconsciously. I have encountered many stereotypes when speaking about neurodivergence. This book started and will end with a meeting with public sector managers who each had their own spoken or unspoken stereotypes. Do all autistic people love technology? Are all ADHD'ers flighty and likely to move jobs frequently? Can I trust this critical report to a dyslexic manager?

A common misconception I have encountered is that neurodivergent people are anti-social. Differences in communication styles, and social anxiety with new people and unfamiliar situations can sometimes lead to avoidance of gatherings. In one case, a well-intentioned employer with neurodivergent staff wanted to foster a sense of connection and community. They arranged a Friday lunch meet up and promoted it though their neurodivergent community and other neurodivergent individuals in the area. Weeks went by and, despite the promise of free pizza, few came. Then, Simon, an autistic man who was among the handful of regulars, suggested that others might be more comfortable with an activity, rather than the prospect of navigating unstructured small talk. The employer purchased a video game console and within a month they needed a bigger room as weekly attendance swelled.

Another common stereotype I hear that that neurodivergent people can't lead. This is a somewhat baffling stereotype. There are well-known examples of neurodivergent entrepreneurs and leaders across many fields. Sir Richard Branson, for example, who is dyslexic, or Elon Musk, who told the world he was autistic, opting to use the term Aspergers on the TV show *Saturday Night Live* (O'Kane, 2021; Schwantes, 2018). Ikea was famously founded by Ingvar Kamprad, who used strange names for products because his dyslexia made working with traditional inventory numbers challenging (Wood, 2022).

In the military, UK Vice Admiral Nick Hine went public with his autism diagnosis in 2021. He attributes his success in the military to his blunt communication style (Brown, 2021).

Stereotypes such as neurodivergent people don't make good leaders or are only suited to careers in technology are false and limiting to the potential of your workplace. I have lost count of the times employers have either openly stated or inferred these stereotypes. Inclusive leaders are conscious that stereotypes exist but make a deliberate effort to suspend judgement and look at individuals, their skills, and their interests, not their label. Furthermore, inclusive leaders can take action to level the playing field of opportunity for neurodivergent workers through interventions we will now explore.

Invisibility

Once employed, neurodivergent employees can excel in their area of expertise but fail to progress within an organisation at the same pace as their neurotypical colleagues. Research shows that employees can progress in their careers through behaviours such as being vocal in meetings, networking at events, building relationships with leaders, or volunteering for additional responsibilities (Forret and Dougherty, 2004). Neurodivergent employees can struggle in situations like team meetings and social networking events where neurotypical people thrive. Autistic staff can struggle with unstructured social interactions, while ADHD'ers like me find it difficult to sit still through lengthy presentations and are easily distracted. (Omoigui, 2022).

At an event in 2018, our team presented to an audience of several hundred business and political leaders. The stakes were high! We were pitching for funding to expand our business, while competing with several other worthy organisations for attention and capital. You would be forgiven for thinking that this event was not the ideal situation for some of our neurodivergent staff. At the time we had several autistic staff, many of whom presented with social anxiety and sensory sensitivities.

We took it as a challenge to carve out an opportunity for all our staff to participate and be seen if they wished. While some declined the invitation, Ed, who is autistic, with coexisting sensory processing disorder, volunteered to participate.

Ed is extremely shy, fiercely competitive, and highly intelligent. With his input we decided to set up a game table in the middle of the event. It was a gamble. We knew Ed loved a range of puzzle-based games and no one in our office could beat him, ever. These games provided an opportunity for Ed to demonstrate his skills, while participating in an event he would typically avoid. The gamble paid off, Ed thrived and, as anticipated, dominated all challengers. He even managed to crack jokes (or "sledge", as we say in Australia) anyone who stepped up for a game.

Inclusive leaders who take time to understand the challenges neurodivergent staff face can design meetings and events in a way that enables true participation and an opportunity to be seen. Simple hacks suggested in Chapter 5, such as agendas for meetings, can be extended to events, providing an opportunity for neurodivergent staff to participate in novel ways, like Ed's example. Writing, either before, during, or after meetings or events through email, live polls, or instant messaging, can allow more ideas and feedback to be heard.

Confidence

We have likely all worked or studied with people who exude confidence. Research shows that confident employees receive greater compensation and advance more quickly in their careers than colleagues with less confidence. A University of Melbourne study found that "those who self-reported higher levels of confidence earlier in school earned better wages and were promoted more quickly" (University of Melbourne, 2012).

This disparity can have a particularly significant impact on neu-rodivergent employees. While neurodivergent people may be excellent workers and excel in their area of expertise, self-promotion may not come naturally, even in situations where it is expected, such as interviews and meetings with senior manag-ers. Linda is one such example. Having worked as a project man-ager for several years, Linda was asked to step up and take on the role of project director after the incumbent left for another role. Linda relished her new responsibility, and after four months as the acting product director was formally interviewed for the role. In Linda's own words, she works much better than she inter-views, where she lacks confidence and gets incredibly nervous. Despite years of good performance and acting in the very role she was being interviewed for, Linda was a wreck during the interview. Unable to provide answers to scenario-based ques-tions, Linda panicked and became flush with embarrassment. The employer passed over Linda for the role and hired an out-sider. Linda resigned shortly after and has gone onto establish her own firm.

An inclusive leader should distinguish between overconfident workers with low abilities and underconfident workers with high abilities. This comes through getting to know your staff and monitoring their productivity. In Luke's company, profiled earlier in this chapter, staff are judged by their output, not what they say they have done. If someone is hugely talented but is held back by their lack of confidence, they can be helped by mentoring or having a senior leader advocate for them.

Networks

Have you heard the phrase, it is not what you know but who you know? While often related to getting a start in an organisation, it is equally true for advancement. Once employed, those who are able to expand their networks, particularly with senior leaders, build social capital (Adler and Kwon, 2002). My parents often used the phrase and encouraged me when I started my career to make friends at all levels. Thankfully, I was mature enough to listen to their advice and found that networking comes naturally to me. Employees who skilfully network and establish a favourable reputation and relationships with peers and senior leaders are able to learn about job openings, stretch assignments, or gain advantages in promotions (Chanland and Murphy, 2018).

Access to networks is not evenly distributed for staff starting their careers or leaders looking to advance. Research suggests that diverse leaders face structural barriers to advancement, such as lack of access to informal networks and lack of role models. Diverse leaders also face perception barriers, such as negative stereotyping and evaluation against a White male leadership standard (Chanland and Murphy, 2018).

Many neurodivergent employees, especially those with difficulties navigating social networks, are unlikely to develop broad networks without structured support and programmes to facilitate introductions. Despite their promise, even the best-intentioned employee value propositions can still result in some employees missing out on the promised workplace benefits. Risks remain that neurodivergent employees will continue to be overlooked for promotion, fail to advance at the same pace as neurotypical colleagues, and either stagnate in their roles, be let go, or quit.

I started writing *Untapped Talent* with a view to equip employers with practical advice on how to attract and advance neurodivergent talent. Indeed, most of my professional focus in the last eight years has been exactly that. However, as I have researched and spoken with neurodivergent individuals and employers around the world, I have realised that there is more to be done within workplaces, with existing neurodivergent staff, managers, and allies.

To break the glass ceiling for neurodivergent employees, inclusive leaders must take deliberate steps to ensure that everyone feels safe to speak up, contribute their skills, and reach their potential. Outlined below are interventions that inclusive leaders can implement to address the uneven access to the benefits of an employee value proposition.

1. **Visibility – start with data.** We live and work in an age of unprecedented access to data and analysis tools, so why not use them? To see how your employees are communicating and collaborating, consider social network analysis to understand the connections among employees and determine who is in the in group, and who is being overlooked. The use of data analysis tools such as those offered by Culture Amp or Worklytics can extend to measuring output.

2. **Transparency, open systems for progression.** In Luke's company, the output of employees is clearly measured against transparent criteria for evaluation and advancement.

Everyone in Luke's company knows exactly what they must do to show that they are ready to progress. Your workplace may not have the budget for enterprise productivity software, but you could start by openly sharing key performance indicators and results by teams and employees each reporting period.

3. **Regular feedback.** Traditional performance management which includes annual performance reviews, key performance indicators, and 360-degree feedback surveys, can feel like a job interview all over again. The process is formal, documented, and often involves HR business partners who may have little interaction with individual managers and staff throughout the year. While it is important for workplaces to have a system to evaluate and record performance, neurodivergent employees and managers will both benefit from frequent feedback. In fact, more regular feedback through the year is likely to benefit every employee and manager. Having experienced performance management as an employee and manager, I can say that there is room for improvement. The end of quarter or yearly review should not be a surprise. As a guide, if new information is being introduced in a formal performance review, then the staff, manager, and feedback system have failed.

4. **Inclusive leadership.** As previously covered, leaders profoundly impact the employee experience. Leaders can model inclusion through their behaviours and decisions. One way that leaders can demonstrate inclusion is by offering stretch assignments to the quietest members of the team (when the assignment matches an employee's skills and development goals). For best effect, provide advance

warning rather than putting someone on the spot in a meeting.

5. **Reverse mentorship.** Neurodivergent staff have much to teach a workplace and its leaders. I would like to see more workplaces adopting a reverse mentorship programme. The programme could match a senior leader with neurodivergent staff, with the purpose of mutual education and connection. Leaders would learn first hand what improvements could be made through the employee lifecycle, company products, and services. Neurodivergent staff would benefit from relationships with senior leaders which build social capital and enhance networks.

Separation
Constructive offboarding practices

Employee turnover is a natural part of the employee lifecycle, and something every workplace and employee will navigate. The rates of employee turnover, or attrition as it is sometimes called, vary by industry and can be influenced by seasonality, advancements in technology, or global events such as the Covid-19 pandemic – the last of these giving rise to the so-called "Great Resignation", which led to record number of people quitting their jobs in 2021 (Sull, Sull and Zweig, 2022).

According to AHRI (2023, p. 5), the "12-month employee turnover rate to the end of April 2023 is currently 12%, with 20% of organisations reporting annual turnover of 20% and above".

Whatever the externalities or industry you operate in, opportunities exist to improve the separate phase of the employee lifecycle. Understanding and managing this turnover effectively is crucial for maintaining a healthy workplace, particularly when it involves neurodivergent employees who can find any change especially hard to navigate. We will consider voluntary separation where an employee leaves a workplace to accept another position, moves interstate or overseas, or retires. Involuntary separation occurs in circumstances where an employee is terminated because of poor performance, or the redundancy of their position.

There is industry evidence to suggest that neurodivergent employees in dedicated work programmes enjoy longer tenure. For example, neurodivergent employees at EY, SAP, JPMorgan Chase, and Microsoft – which run four of the largest U.S. autism hiring programmes – report a retention rate of more than 90 per cent (Culture Amp, 2024). However, there is little research on the average tenure of neurodivergent employees in open employment. This may be due to the chronic lack of disclosure and reliable data on how employees identify. It is safe to assume that many of your neurodivergent employees, those you know about, anyway, are going to leave for another job or due to a change in life such as retirement.

When a neurodivergent employee decides to leave voluntarily, it is important to handle the process with sensitivity and transparency to ensure a smooth transition. In Chapter 4 we covered recruitment, where important principles of clear communication and transparency of process were recommended. We can adopt the same principles to the separation stage.

§   **Clear communication:** Schedule a conversation to understand the employee's rationale for leaving and gather feedback. This feedback can provide valuable insights for improving workplace practices and retaining talent.

§   **Structured information:** Provide a clear outline of the resignation process, including timelines and next steps. If the resignation process is not formally documented, this is a great opportunity to start. Your neurodivergent and neurotypical staff and managers will thank you. A clear structured process reduces anxiety associated with ambiguity and helps the employee feel more in control. Be clear about what is expected during this process; remember explicit instructions are recommended.

§   **Career transition support:** Offer resources such as job placement services or referrals to external recruitment agencies if the employee is leaving without a confirmed role. Supporting their next career step shows a commitment to their future success and will be noticed by remaining staff.

§   **Emotional and mental health support:** Go beyond statutory requirements by offering access to mental health resources. Change such as leaving a job can be stressful even when it is chosen voluntarily, and additional support can help ease the transition.

Before we progress to cover involuntary separation, it is worth unpacking Rejection Sensitivity Dysphoria (RSD) which is particularly common in autistic and ADHD individuals. RSD is an extreme emotional reaction. It can be triggered by the perception of rejection or criticism by someone important in the individual's life. It can also occur if an individual falls short of their own standards (Dodson, 2020).

While RSD isn't an officially recognised medical condition, neuro-divergent people, particularly ADHD'ers, report feelings of intense emotional pain (Cleveland Clinic, 2024). As Marshall (2024) states, "An important aspect of RSD that is not often spoken about is that we tend to have a very critical inner voice – this is like having your worst enemy living inside your brain, continually berating you. When we then receive an external criticism or rejection from someone, we react so deeply to it because it seems to 'confirm' the stream of criticism we are already receiving from this inner voice."

It is unlikely that any workplace will know if their neurodivergent staff have RSD. The individuals themselves may not know. Therefore, it is important that employers handle separation with empathy, patience, and fairness.

Separation, either voluntary or involuntary, is a time of change and can be stressful for the individual who is leaving, their manager, and the staff who remain. Handling the separation process for neurodivergent employees with a deep understanding of their unique needs can limit stress and ensure a respectful and professional exit process. This not only benefits the departing employee but also reinforces a workplace's commitment to inclusive and compassionate leadership which will be remembered long after an employee leaves.

The following are practical suggestions for managing separation that occurs involuntarily.

Involuntary separation: managing performance-related exits and redundancy

§   **Performance-related separation:**

o   **Transparent communication:** Clearly document and communicate performance issues well before reaching the point of termination. Provide constructive feedback and clarity on successful performance requirements, and offer ample opportunities for improvement. Refer to the suggestions for regular feedback above and don't wait for an annual performance review to raise concerns.

o   **Supportive measures:** Wherever possible, implement support measures such as additional training or adjustments to the work environment to help the employee meet performance expectations.

o   **Compassionate delivery:** If termination is necessary, conduct the discussion in a private setting, explaining the decision respectfully and empathetically. Provide clear and explicit feedback and offer suggestions for improvement for future roles. Follow up the meeting with written confirmation, and provide a clear outline of the redundancy process, including timelines and next steps.

§   **Redundancy:**

o   **Clear rationale:** Provide a clear explanation of the business reasons behind the redundancy to help the employee understand the situation. Wherever possible, include the big picture; the more information the better.

o **Fair compensation and support:** Offer a fair redundancy package and include career transition support and mental health resources to aid their adjustment. Depending on which country you are operating in there will be legislation that covers employee entitlements at separation. Your HR business partner or legal council should be able to assist with this.

o **Structured communication:** Hold a one-on-one meeting to discuss the redundancy, ensuring transparency and allowing the employee to ask questions. Follow up the meeting with written confirmation, and provide a clear outline of the redundancy process, including timelines and next steps.

o **Emotional and mental health support:** Go beyond statutory requirements by offering access to mental health resources. Change, such as leaving a job, can be stressful, especially when occurring involuntarily, and additional support can help ease the transition.

We have now covered the employee lifecycle, from attraction to separation. The next two chapters will cover disclosure throughout the employment lifecycle, and the business case for neuroinclusion, where I will introduce benefits for both entire organisations and individual teams.

7

Disclosure throughout the employment lifecycle

Man is least himself when he talks in his own person.
Give him a mask, and he will tell you the truth.

Oscar Wilde

The masks we wear

Have you heard the phrase "bring your whole self" to work? It's a modern cliché that can form part of an employer's value proposition. As employers continue to prioritise diversity and inclusion within their workplace (Dixon-Fyle et al., 2020), there has been a growing recognition of the importance of disclosure of personal characteristics, such as sexuality and disability, in fostering a sense of belonging among employees.

Disclosure of these personal characteristics can be a difficult and personal decision for individuals, as it involves revealing potentially sensitive or private information. However, disclosure can be an important factor in promoting a sense of belonging in the workplace. One reason why disclosure can be important is that it allows employees to be their authentic selves at work, rather than feeling the need to hide or mask certain aspects of their identity. This can create a more welcoming and inclusive work environment, where employees feel comfortable and supported in being their true selves. Disclosure can also help to create a sense of connection and solidarity among employees, as it allows individuals to share their experiences, strengths, and challenges with others who may have similar backgrounds or experiences. This can foster a sense of community and support within the workplace, which can in turn promote a sense of belonging.

However, available data tends to indicate that most employees do not disclose a non-apparent or invisible disability. One report estimated that 1–2 per cent of employees disclosed a disability on the Voluntary Self-Identification of Disability form that is commonly used across organisations in the United States (Santuzzi, Martinez and Keating, 2022). Among white-collar workers, a 2017 study from the Centre for Talent Innovation revealed only 3.2 per cent of employees voluntarily disclose their disability status, or self-identify as having a disability to their employers. The same survey showed 30 per cent of employees identified as having a disability (Sherbin et al., 2017). The consequences of concealing ones neurodivergence in the workplace can be detrimental to health and work performance (Mellifont, 2021).

What I have been wrestling with is why so many people choose not to disclose. This comes from personal experience as someone identifying as neurodivergent who chose not to disclose for decades. Many of the neurodivergent individuals I have spoken with have at one point or another hidden their condition from an employer. Some describe the risk they feel in disclosing, others are intensely private and choose to keep this personal information out of the workplace. Disclosure can differ depending on the stage of an employee lifecycle and is also influenced by cultural background, gender, and the maturity of an individual's neurodivergent identity. To follow are two scenarios for your consideration in terms of their messages about the need for safe disclosure throughout the employment lifecycle.

There is something about Marvin

Marvin had a smile so brilliant you could read a book by it. Tall, confident, and skilled at his job, Marvin was a joy to manage. Reports were in on time, customers loved working with him, and Marvin's team considered him among our most valuable contributors. I miss working with Marvin; we would often travel together to see clients, and that incidental time can accelerate a relationship. Marvin eventually took his glowing references and winning smile to a bigger field, landing a regional role with a global tech company.

Years went past, Marvin got married, started a postgraduate degree, and I moved interstate. We kept in contact as best you can in modern life. I took some pride in his career accelerating. In reality, I had little to do with his progress.

Early one Monday morning I noticed Marvin had been profiled by the university he was completing a Master's degree with. In the LinkedIn post, Marvin had thanked the university, his employer, and family. Then, to my surprise, he attributed his success to the unique way his mind works. Marvin is dyslexic. I had to read the introduction a couple times, pausing over the words dyslexic and neurodivergent.

I felt a sense of loss and curiosity in equal measure. I reached out to Marvin's Executive Assistant and we arranged a time to speak.

I started our conversation with a simple question. Marvin and I had spent years working together, both not knowing the other is neurodivergent. I had kept my ADHD diagnosis a closely guarded secret, as Marvin had his dyslexia. Why? "I was ashamed" was Marvin's immediate response, expanding to say that he didn't want to give people a reason to doubt him. Having struggled terribly at school, Marvin was determined not to take that legacy into his career.

Marvin feared that managers would assume his written communication would be negatively impacted by dyslexia. These negative perceptions could impact the types of work assignments he was given and his prospects for advancement. The reality is Marvin has a gift with numbers and how he structures data, along with a strong work ethic.

Since publicly disclosing his diagnosis Marvin has received a range of responses. Some were surprised, others encouraged, and a few were unintentionally patronising. Marvin recalled that a senior manager had expressed admiration for him completing his studies and advancing in the company, "in spite of his condition". It warmed my heart to hear that Marvin had corrected the manager, saying his owes his success to hard work and to his dyslexia. Marvin went on to share that the way his mind categorises information is an advantage. I doubt I would have had the same level of courage in a similar scenario.

I have reflected since our conversation. If Marvin and I had had a different level of relationship and if we had known about each other's neurodivergence, would it have changed anything about how we worked, our mutual trust, and what tasks Marvin was assigned?

The reality is neurodivergence was not spoken about in our workplace, ever. Like Marvin, I feared that seeds of doubt about my ability would have been sown had I disclosed. The environment was competitive, male-dominated, and homogenous. At the time it may also have come across as irrelevant, as neurodiversity simply was not a part of the conversation. If it's not being spoken about, and no one is asking, why would you tell?

Not so different

Magda is on a mission to show employers that neurodivergent people are not so different to everyone else. But for Magda's mission, timing is everything. Like a growing number of women, Magda was diagnosed in her 30s following the diagnosis of her child. Years later Magda continues to learn how her autism and ADHD combine, while unlearning masking practices which were leaving her exhausted at the end of each workday.

Having studied organisational psychology, Magda set off building a career in HR and talent acquisition. She says her colleagues and friends would describe her as quirky. I didn't see this but perhaps Magda doesn't consider me a friend or was still masking when we meet. Now, more than a decade after starting her career and several years following her diagnosis, Magda is retrospectively attributing career success to her neurodivergence. Magda wants employers to know that in the right environment neurodivergent people have advantages, like creativity and the ability to hyperfocus. However, Magda won't share her diagnosis with employers right away.

Years of being misinterpreted have forced Magda to develop a concise and repeatable method of communicating. It has also turned Magda into a detective who is constantly trying to understand the truth behind whatever is said. Magda focuses on why something is said and often considers numerous possibilities. This curiosity has proven valuable in HR and talent roles where there is conflict or blockages in a process. Through the trauma of being misinterpreted, Magda has developed a people systems skillset which has proven invaluable in her career and personal life.

When working, most of Magda's meetings are over the phone or via video conference. Whenever speaking, Magda refers to speaking notes, so she values agendas for meetings to allow preparation. Magda's colleagues report that her follow-up notes are timely, concise, and easy to understand. Magda's personal need for structure is a blessing for the wider team as they benefit from a rich history of past meetings that can be easily referred to.

Not every workplace is created equal. Through her career Magda has experienced diverse workplace cultures where difference was celebrated and some she would like to forget. In all but one workplace Magda has chosen not to disclose her neurodivergence through the recruitment process. At the time of meeting, the labour market was highly competitive and Magda didn't want to give an employer a reason to doubt her. "Neurodivergence is still misunderstood, I don't want an employer's bias holding me back." Magda does feel a "sense of responsibility" to share her neurodivergence but has chosen to first show her value before telling her story. Knowing Magda, the timing of her starting a new role, showing value, and then sharing her neurodivergent identity won't be too far apart!

Factors impacting on disclosure through the employment lifecycle

While the choices for Marvin or Magda to disclose is entirely theirs, critical factors in stages throughout the employment lifecycle can influence such decisions. These factors are raised as follows.

Recruitment and disclosure of neurodivergence

In an employment lifecycle the first opportunity for an individual to disclose is through the application process, often in the context of offering support and adjustments. Many employers now include a sentence at the end of a job description to encourage disclosure. Here is one example from the global advisory firm Ernst & Young (EY).

> Diversity, equity, and inclusiveness (DE&I) are core to who we are, how we work and how we live our values. We hold a collective commitment to continue to drive an environment where all differences are valued, practices are equitable, and everyone experiences a sense of belonging – where people are inspired to team and lead inclusively in their interactions every day. We encourage applications from people of all ages, nationalities, abilities, cultures, sexual orientations, and gender identities

and are committed to providing an equitable and barrier free recruitment experience for all. We encourage you to share any support and adjustments you need to be your best and participate equitably in our recruitment process. We understand sharing your needs with us can be daunting, so if you have questions before or during your application, we welcome you to get in touch at … (Ernst and Young, 2024)

In this example, EY acknowledges the challenge in disclosing personal information. However, as (Santuzzi, Martinez and Keating, 2022) explain, self-reporting lays the responsibility at the feet of the candidate, by relying on self-report identification. Workers with disabilities can feel uncomfortable and uncertain on how to respond to disability disclosure forms (Santuzzi, Martinez and Keating, 2022).

Further limitations of asking for disclosure through the recruitment process stem from neurodivergent candidates who fear discrimination, social stigma, and negative work consequences. One study found individuals were concerned about negative consequences of disclosure, including lowered expectations, isolation from co-workers, and being passed over for promotion (Von Schrader, Malzer and Bruyère, 2014).

In addition, candidates may not be aware of what types of adjustments are even available. I am still working out what I need to be successful at work, decades after my diagnosis. In Chapter 4, we covered what changes employers can make through recruitment phase. To account for individuals who may not know what adjustments they require, start by including a list of common adjustments at the end of the job description. Better yet, critically re-evaluate current recruitment processes to be less rigid and with more options for flexibility for all candidates – this will likely be more inclusive and beneficial for both neurodivergent and neurotypical candidates.

Advancement and disclosure of neurodivergence

When seeking an internal promotion, Maria, an ambitious and highly qualified neurodivergent professional, said she didn't want to give the hiring manager a single reason not to promote her. Hence, she made the choice to keep her autism and anxiety hidden. This is not surprising as negative stereotypes wrongly associate disability with low competence in the workplace (Santuzzi, Martinez and Keating, 2022). Maria's concern is well founded. As a woman in a technical field, Maria has already battled negative stereotypes her whole career. Researchers suggest that "The concern about negative performance stereotypes might be especially threatening to workers who already face systemic discrimination and negative performance stereotypes due to other identities, such as gender, race, age or ethnicity" (Santuzzi, Martinez and Keating, 2022, p. 476).

Taylor, an African American woman working in New Zealand for a PR firm, said she already feels different enough without sharing her recent ADHD diagnosis. Taylor described the pressure of compounded difference, where multiple and intersecting identities amplify daily challenges. This leads Taylor to a conscious choice to camouflage her neurodivergent behaviour in the workplace, a practice she describes as mentally and emotionally exhausting.

As a result, Taylor is selective about when to share her neurodivergence, most often when it's already a part of the conversation and relevant.

The reasons why people have not shared their neurodivergence are varied, and yet, quite understandable. However, I have noticed change happening as an educated understanding of neurodivergence expands throughout workplaces. Sharing neurodivergence, while personal, can be deeply advantageous for both the person and the employer in a workplace to more fully understand each other, and to better leverage the strengths that may come from it. Disclosures will increase, provided there is sufficient trust and understanding to embrace all that it entails.

Performance management and disclosure of neurodivergence

One worrying trend I am noticing is employees disclosing their neurodivergence at the point of performance management. If disclosures have not occurred before performance management processes kick in, it can create extra stress and complexity for both the employee and employer.

This formal process, often facilitated by a HR business partner, involves setting goals, evaluating progress, and providing feedback to improve employee performance. Several neurodivergent employees and managers I have spoken with have cited poorly communicated change, return-to-office mandates, and organisation restructures as factors leading to increased workplace stress. These scenarios can be triggers for a decrease in workplace performance that can be sudden and dramatic.

One manager navigating a scenario of an underperforming employee who disclosed they were autistic said they felt they had failed as an organisation. In their case the employee's disclosure of autism through a formal performance management process led to a protracted, stressful, and costly scenario that might have been avoided. This scenario highlights the risks for workplaces who fail to create a supportive environment and fully understand their workers' needs.

Georgia is late

Monday's meeting began as the countless before. For the first 10 minutes of the weekly 1-hour operations meeting the team essentially caught up with each other's news. Sarah's son had a birthday party on the weekend, the photos revealed the theme was Minecraft. Newcastle had defeated Manchester United which was bad news for many in the office tipping competition. Holidays were being planned, Netflix shows were recommended and cafés were rubbished. Then, as usual, Georgia joined the call, at 9.10 a.m. "Afternoon, Georgia, glad you could make it", sniped her manager. Some giggled, Georgia looked unfazed.

Georgia excelled at her job, she is organised, efficient, and widely trusted. Georgia possesses excellent attention to detail, often picking up on errors that others have missed. These traits served her and the organisation well. As a contract manager, Georgia was responsible for ensuring suppliers delivered to the contract specifications. Not much was known about Georgia away from the office; unlike her colleagues, she seldom shared personal news.

One fact that Georgia had skilfully guarded is that she is autistic. While diagnosis rates among women are on the rise, much of what we know about autism is based on the presentation of men. Georgia, like many women, had become adept at masking at work. Masking, as we have learned, is the practice of learning the behaviour of non-autistic people as a way of fitting in. In Georgia's case she has learnt how to laugh at short stories that end abruptly causing others to chuckle. Others may call these short stories jokes. While Georgia can't see anything funny in what is said, she understands others do and the typical response is to laugh.

Months passed and the same pattern continued, Monday meetings, late Georgia. You could almost set your watch to it. The tipping point came when Georgia started dialling in late to supplier briefings. Fortnightly calls were an important part of contract management and being late for these was the final straw for manager Rohit to have a "talk". HR became involved and a performance improvement plan was formalised. While nothing about Georgia's job performance could be questioned, the perception grew that Georgia was unorganised and, worse, uncommitted to her role.

For someone who prides themselves on work outcomes, the performance improvement process was devastating. Georgia was sleeping worse than normal, eating infrequently, and constantly worried. It was at this crisis point that Georgia took the brave decision to share her diagnosis, first with HR and then with Rohit. It was a watershed moment. Counter to her growing reputation, she was neither unorganised nor uncommitted. The truth is Georgia felt uncomfortable navigating small talk. The first 10 minutes of team meetings and now supplier briefings were confusing, uncomfortable, and frankly, according to Georgia, pointless. Georgia dreaded being put on the spot. Most of the conversation revolved around children, which she didn't have, or sports she knew existed but had no interest in. So, to avoid stress and potential embarrassment, Georgia, against everything she knew about professionalism, started joining late. When Georgia's tardiness was met with humour, ambivalence, or silence she assumed it was not a big deal, until suddenly it was.

Two avoidable practices led to this unnecessary and stressful situation. Firstly, a lack of clear communication on the expectations of being on time to meetings. Putting Georgia on the spot with attempted humour may have appeared to others as a clear message of expectations but it wasn't to her. Secondly, Georgia's manager and her colleagues displayed a distinct lack of curiosity. Everyone assumed Georgia arriving late was just her lack of organisation or, the more dangerous thought, a lack of commitment. At no point did anyone take the time to find out why. It may have taken some digging and patience for those enquiring, but Georgia assures me she would have explained the deliberate avoidance of small talk.

Georgia may have also shared that, like many autistic people, she has lower than average verbal processing, meaning it is more difficult for her to comprehend verbal conversations. Especially when multiple people are speaking at the same time. Something neurotypical people tend to do all the time, according to Georgia. Research has shown that autistic individuals experience challenges with complex verbal information, particularly when tasks require discrimination of speech sounds or understanding of semantic content. These difficulties become more pronounced with the increasing complexity of verbal stimuli and tasks (Key and D'Ambrose Slaboch, 2021).

Fast forward 18 months and Georgia couldn't be happier in her workplace. She continues to use her razor-sharp attention to detail to avoid project creep. She has even taken on a stretch assignment exploring the use of Large Language Models like ChatGPT to analyse contracts. What has made the difference is an overwhelming feeling of being understood coupled with some small modifications to team meetings. Georgia now dials in at 9.05 and has taken responsibility for taking minutes and ensuring each meeting sticks to time. Ironic for someone once thought to have poor time management skills.

Furthermore, the team have trialled something unique. Once a month they have scripted catch-up for the first 10 minutes of a meeting. Talking points are circulated the Thursday prior and the Zoom breakout rooms used for discussion. Like many organisations that adapted quickly to the arrival of Covid-19, team meetings are exclusively via Zoom. The last Monday of the month's meeting is cameras off, voices muted, and text chat only. Georgia loves it, she can type fast and is no longer overwhelmed by comprehending multiple voices speaking at once. The extroverts who normally fill every silence with their voices are getting used to it.

While the adaptations Georgia's team have embraced are an example of inclusive leadership, the question needs to be asked, was there anything about the work environment that led Georgia to keep her diagnosis to herself for many years? Georgia's manager Rohit and close colleagues felt disappointed in themselves. Was there anything among their culture, leadership, or relationships that kept Georgia from disclosing?

What can employers do to encourage safe disclosure of neurodivergence throughout the employment lifecycle?

To be successful in any endeavour you need to attract and retain good people like Marvin, Magda, and Georgia. I will now focus on what employers can do to build inclusive workplace cultures where neurodivergent employees can be seen and be themselves.

Psychological safety

When considering what employers can do to create inclusive workplace cultures, one concept lays the foundation – this concept being psychological safety. Amy Edmondson's much-loved work argues that psychological safety is the collective understanding that one's team is an environment safe for interpersonal risk-taking. "Team psychological safety involves but goes beyond interpersonal trust; it describes a team climate characterised by interpersonal trust and mutual respect in which people are comfortable being themselves" (Edmondson, 1999).

The concept of psychological safety surfaces frequently in my conversations with neurodivergent individuals. One of the most common hopes I hear when speaking with neurodivergent individuals is finding a job where they can "be themselves". One jobseeker recently told me they wanted to work in an environment where they didn't have to pretend to be someone else.

Leaders who foster psychological safety and maintain genuine relationships with their teams have a significant influence on disclosure. As Von Schrader, Malzer and Bruyère (2014) found, workplace culture, employers' commitment to disability inclusion, as well as an employee's relationship with their supervisor were important factors encouraging disclosure. Individuals were more likely to disclose disabilities where they enjoyed a positive and supportive relationship with their direct manager.

Educate and celebrate

Author and political and disability advocate Helen Keller once wrote "the highest result of education is tolerance" (Keller, 1926, p. 39).

Education plays a critical role for managers and allies who can be cautious about approaching topics that are unfamiliar to them. In my experience working with employers, education erodes the biggest barrier to inclusion, fear. This idea was captured in the 2017 Centre for Talent innovation global survey. A respondent from the UK stated, "One of the things that really struck me is that people are frightened to ask questions. They don't know the right language or terminology. So they tend to avoid the conversation altogether, all because they don't want to cause offence" (Sherbin et al., 2017, p. 20).

Accenture's 2021 survey found that in organisations that provided accessible inclusion training designed to help employees with disabilities thrive, staff are 35 per cent more likely to disclose their disabilities (Henneborn, 2021). Education is the cornerstone for shaping community and workplace perceptions. Workplace education on neurodiversity and disability can play a pivotal role in reducing stigma and encouraging disclosure, ultimately fostering a sense of belonging among employees.

Model from the top

Earlier in this chapter we heard about Marvin and the revealing conversation we had following his disclosure of dyslexia. In the competitive, male-dominated, and homogenous workplace in which we found ourselves, every leader fit the mould. There were few female leaders. Most senior leaders were men, and none identified as having a disability, or any discernible difference for that matter. While it was never measured, it's likely that this environment had low psychological safety.

In contrast, one employer I have enjoyed working alongside takes deliberate measures to model difference among its leaders. The firm, a global payment services provider, benefits from a diverse workforce with multiple senior leaders identifying as having a disability. The Global Head of Human Resources told me a key area of focus is hiring and advancing neurodivergent staff. At least one leader identities as autistic and openly shares their experience with anyone interested in listening. The office has adapted to a range of working styles and introduced a quiet room and fidget toys in meeting rooms. Recently the fidget toys have made appearances in interviews, where hiring managers talk about their use in an effort to normalise use. These small actions have led to the firm being recognised with industry awards, and they report lower turnover and higher staff engagement than the industry average.

The Accenture survey found that "when employees with disabilities have role models at the leadership level who have disclosed their own disabilities, they are 15% more likely to have higher career aspirations than their peers in other organizations. And with this factor in place, employees are 26% more likely to be open about their disability" (Henneborn, 2021).

Researchers also found that disclosure was influenced when individuals with a disability succeed in the workplace. Employers can cultivate a culture that encourages disclosure by promoting successes of workers with disabilities, in an authentic and genuine way (Von Schrader, Malzer and Bruyère, 2014). The saying "you can't be what you can't see" is a commonly used phrase for a reason. Workplaces that take small steps, like the global payment services provider, can yield significant dividends.

Mixed results

The organisational benefits of employees disclosing non-apparent disabilities are well understood and include: fostering a sense of belonging among employees, lower staff turnover, and a reduction in psychological injury. However, the results for individuals are not all positive.

Romualdez, Walker and Remington (2021) studied the experiences of autistic adults disclosing in the workplace. They concluded that disclosure led to mixed outcomes. Participants spoke about having improved mental health and greater well-being after disclosing. "I have become much more open about it because the response to disclosure has always been positive, so I feel able to mask a little less and live more authentically, which is good for the well-being" (Romualdez, Walker and Remington, 2021, p. 6).

For others, disclosure resulted in problematic stereotyping: "… unspoken assumptions, people assuming I'm good at everything because I am good at one thing, and people assuming I am terrible at everything because I am terrible at one thing" (Romualdez, Walker and Remington, 2021, p. 6).

This research mirrors my experience of working with neurodivergent individuals in a range of workplaces. Neurodivergent individuals I have spoken with experience a mixture of outcomes following disclosure. Employer reactions can be overwhelming positive, leading to closer relationships, reduced pressure to mask to fit into neurotypical standards, and a greater feeling of belonging. Unfortunately, many have shared that their disclosure was dismissed, ignored, or, worse, questioned.

Conclusion

Marvin's smile was visible to anyone who met him, unlike his diagnosis, which hid in plain sight. Magda's methodical approach to communication was borne out of being misunderstood. Georgia struggled to fit the mould. Each story underscores a simple truth: when people can be themselves at work, everyone benefits.

Their experiences highlight a crucial point about neurodivergence in the workplace. It's not the act of disclosure itself that matters. What's important is creating a culture where such a conversation is as normal and accepted as discussing weekend plans. This requires a shift in our thinking, from seeing neurodivergence as something to be managed to recognising it as a source of unique skills and perspectives that can lead to better problem-solving and more dynamic teams.

Our collective task is to build cultures where individuals like Marvin, Magda, and Georgia can share their true selves. Where the diverse abilities they bring are not just welcomed but seen as essential for innovation and success.

8
The business case for neuroinclusion

I recently had the opportunity to present the case for neuroinclusion to a group of business leaders. I was to be introduced by a senior leader, Max ahead of a 45-minute presentation. At the end of a flattering introduction Max added one sentence which has stuck with me ever since. "This is a great cause, and we need to all get behind it." At the time I didn't correct the statement, and simply went on with my presentation.

In Chapter 2, we learned that our choice of words matter, as these can have a powerful influence on the beliefs and actions of others. Anchoring neuroinclusion to charity demonstrates a medical or deficit view of neurodivergent people. This view holds that neurodivergent people need our help, rather than we as employers need theirs! In hindsight this was a missed opportunity to state my belief that neuroinclusion is not a charitable act. As we will see throughout this chapter, incorporating diversity and inclusion into the workforce is sound people and business practice.

This chapter will cover:

- The business case for diversity and inclusion;

- Common challenges for attaining diversity in the workplace;
- The diversity dividend for teams; and
- The cost of doing nothing.

The business case for diversity and inclusion

There is a large body of evidence supporting the business case for diversity and inclusion. Herring (2009, p. 220) states that "a diverse workforce is good for business, offering a direct return on investment and promising greater corporate profits and earnings". Why do diverse workforces outperform homogeneous ones? One reason is diversity of thought drives innovation; "the most innovative company, must also be the most diverse", says Apple Inc. (Bourke and Dillon, 2018, p. 84).

Praslova (2024) argues there are two cases for inclusion that need not be mutually exclusive. The human case centres on the moral and ethical arguments for creating diverse and inclusive environments, while the business case focuses on the tangible benefits, like attracting diverse talent, improving creativity, decision-making, and reputation, leading to increased profits (Praslova, 2024, p. 185).

Global consulting firm McKinsey has studied diversity in the workplace for several years. Their 2020 study included data from 1,000 large employers across 15 countries including the United States, Brazil, and Japan. McKinsey's research concluded that diverse teams are more likely to be radically innovative and be able to anticipate future consumer needs (Dixon-Fyle et al.,

2020). Companies with higher gender and ethnic diversity are more likely to financially outperform their peers.

- Companies in the top quartile for gender diversity on executive teams were 25 per cent more likely to experience above average profitability than those in the fourth quartile.
- Companies in the top quartile for ethnic diversity on executive teams were 36 per cent more likely to experience above average profitability than those in the fourth quartile.

These statistics, while helpful in laying the foundational argument for diversity, are narrow in their focus on the differences we can see, such as gender and ethnicity. As Nobel Prize winner Richard Thaler argues, in addition to racial and gender diversity, it is important to consider diversity of thought (Javetski and Koller, 2018).

The business case for a greater representation of neurodivergence in the workplace can also be argued along moral grounds: the imperative to employ underrepresented people to better reflect the wider society that organisations operate within. Other arguments include access to a broader talent pool with skills such as attention to detail, visual thinking, pattern recognition, and creativity (Mahto, Sniderman and Hogan, 2022).

In Chapter 4 we learned recruitment tactics from neuroinclusion leaders in the Autism@Work roundtable. Lessons from Microsoft, SAP, EY and JPMorgan Chase are helpful for any workplace considering their own dedicated hiring programme to attract neurodivergent workers. The business case for neuroinclusion leaders to invest in a hiring programme included:

- Access to untapped talent;

- Focus on accessibility as a core company value;
- The potential for process quality improvements;
- The success of the initial pilot; and
- Reputational gain.

Other notable programmes include the DXC Dandelion Program, which embraces, supports and expands the skills of neurodivergent individuals to help them secure long-term careers in IT. The Dandelion Program boasts a retention rate of 92 per cent and claims their neurodivergent teams are 30–40 per cent more productive than existing teams that are lacking neurodivergence (DXC Technology, 2023). Similarly, the autism hiring programme at JP Morgan Chase found that autistic employees can be up to 140 per cent more productive than neurotypical employees (Praslova, 2024). The programme, which started as a pilot in 2015 with a handful of employees, today spans more than 40 different roles across nine countries, including Argentina, Canada, and England (JPMorgan Chase, 2023).

When business leaders question the return on investment for neuroincluson, my question is this: why would global corporations, operating in highly competitive industries, invest in programmes that don't deliver a business as well as a social return? Furthermore, why would any programme that doesn't deliver returns be expanded beyond the pilot phase? In my opinion, the telling evidence of a solid business case is the expansion of these programmes. The available business case evidence for neuroinclusion is based on dedicated hiring programmes in large corporations. As we will discover, diversity and inclusion are not the same thing, and the type of diversity and the function of roles matters. In researching this book, I have taken time to consider the business case for investing in neuroinclusion education for managers and support for existing neurodivergent staff. Workplaces of all sizes need to ensure they invest in retaining and advancing existing neurodivergent staff.

Common challenges for attaining diversity in the workplace

Diversity and inclusion initiatives can be very hard to get right. Initiatives can be fragmented, reliant on Human Resource teams or Employee Resource Groups (ERG). They often lack executive support or adequate funding. Furthermore, diversity and inclusion initiatives that are not aligned to business strategy will fail to deliver meaningful impact (Dixon-Fyle et al., 2020).

Bell et al. (2011) used meta-analysis to study the link between diversity and team performance, while drilling down into the type of diversity and the type of performance. Functional diversity refers to a variety of work tenure and background within an organisation, such as finance, human resources, marketing, and operations. Bell argues, "A team composed of members from diverse functional backgrounds should have a broader range of perspectives and knowledge to draw on, and they should be able to outperform teams with members from homogenous backgrounds" (Bell et al., 2011, p. 715).

Demographic diversity includes age, gender, and ethnicity. Several critics argue that demographic diversity is linked with increased conflict, lower group cohesiveness, higher absenteeism, and turnover (Herring, 2009). Demographic diversity, when not supported by inclusive leadership or properly integrated into the workplace, can lead to greater intra-group conflict, in turn reducing productivity. One explanation for this is our tendency as humans to classify each other. Social classification theory states that team members classify each other into subgroups. This classification can lead to an in-group and out-group dynamic and a tendency for cooperation within subgroups (Herring, 2009). Inclusive leaders need to be aware of these potential challenges, and assess attitudes towards diversity, monitor team dynamics, and actively manage intra-group conflict.

Diversity was found to be beneficial for creative team performance, where divergent thinking is required to generate many ideas. In contrast, diversity is less helpful when solutions to problems need to be agreed quickly (Bell et al., 2011).

With the business benefits of diversity depending on the type of diversity, the type of team, and the type of leadership, it is little wonder that workplaces don't always get it right and can be slow to start any meaningful initiatives. The following scenario is an example of a disconnect between the stated commitment of diversity from a senior leader, and the responsibility for middle managers to act.

Pressure from the top

The train jolted, then eased away from North Sydney station as I tried to find a quiet row to dial into the meeting. Realising that quiet is a relative concept at 4 p.m. on a weekday I am content with a back corner and noise-cancelling headphones. I rush to set up, laptop, phone, hotspot, ready.

Meanwhile the meeting room was filling up. I check I am on mute as the next station is announced.

It's been three weeks since the first episode of ABC's reality TV programme Employable Me. *The show, an adaptation of a BBC series, follows people with disabilities as they search for their first job. In episode 1 Tim, who is autistic, is interviewed and then hired by Xceptional, the fledgling social enterprise I represent. The weeks that followed are a whirlwind of meetings as hundreds of hungry employers want to hire their Tim.*

Despite my hearing aids turned to max volume I am finding it hard to hear. Blended meetings where some are in the room and others are dialling in rarely work, and this meeting is no exception. We are meeting with the Australian arm of a multi-national investment bank for the first time. What I can pick up is the team is struggling to fill roles in data analytics. Their hiring costs and the time to fill roles are both moving in the wrong direction, and they are scrambling to fix these challenges. Suddenly pressure arrives in a dark blue suit and the meeting changes in an instant. The divisional director was only in the meeting for 15 minutes and we never dealt with them again, but they changed the course of both the conversation that day and our future work with this organisation.

The divisional director had watched the reality TV series, Employable Me, *first alone then with his family. The show had a profound effect and challenged their perceptions of what people with disabilities can achieve. Leaders often do a better job at projecting their voice and I had no problems hearing every word of this speech. The monologue finished with a challenge, the group was going to work with this unproven startup, they were going to change how they hire, and the people in the room were going to make it happen. These directions were accompanied by an outstretched finger as each manager was singled out, as if the pointing was some type of corporate memo.*

Instead of hope and possibility, I saw one emotion on the faces of these managers that would become very familiar in the coming years, fear. As we have seen, there is no shortage of evidence that diversity and inclusion are linked to workplace productivity and innovation. While the evidence at a macro level is clear, the results are mixed when applied to teams.

The diversity dividend for teams

The concept of a diversity dividend "refers to the enhancement in an organisation's performance that is attributable to diversity" (Martins, 2020). An organisation's diversity dividend depends on teams benefiting from diversity. After all, an organisation is made up of many teams.

Every team is different and will be changed when new staff are added or existing members leave. As a starting point, consider the following questions when evaluating a team. It is advisable to ask these questions, through a combination of open discussion, "ask me anything" sessions, and anonymous surveys. Start by looking at the type of team and ask:

- Is it a functional team, or one that requires creativity?
- Is divergent thinking and creativity valued more than convergent thinking and execution?

- What are the observable behaviours and team culture?
- Do team members have agency to do their job well?
- Do team members feel they belong?
- What is the current understanding and lived experience of diversity in general and neurodivergence?
- Are there any spoken or unspoken fears of diversity in general or neurodivergence?
- Are people with lived experience of neurodivergence included in the recruitment process for new team members?

When we started Xceptional in 2017, our focus was getting neurodivergent people into the workplace. There was a view that neurodivergent people were out there, and employers needed to make changes to recognise their skills and accommodate their needs. That work is important and ongoing. More recently, workplaces are realising that they need to better understand neurodivergent staff and neurodivergent customers that they already have.

When evaluating a business case for neuroinclusion at a team level, it is important to make the distinction between: 1. Initiatives to intentionally hire neurodivergent staff; and 2. Initiatives to include existing neurodivergent staff.

The business case for hiring neurodivergent staff will take some to consider and will, as we have learnt, depend on the type of team and its function. However, the case for initiatives such as education, flexible working, and reasonable adjustments that support the inclusion and retainment of existing neurodivergent staff have a rock-solid business case that even the fiercest of critics cannot deny.

The cost of doing nothing

Consider the direct and indirect costs of replacing staff. The cost of replacing an individual employee can vary, ranging from one half to two times the employee's annual salary (McFeely and Wigert, 2019). Employers face direct costs, such as recruitment and training, as well as indirect costs, like productivity loss and declining morale (Alonzo, 2023). In addition to staff turnover, employers in many markets face increased costs and legal requirements to manage both physical and psychological safety.

For example, in 2023, Australia introduced significant changes to workplace health and safety laws, mandating employers to actively manage psychological risks. The new regulations require employers to identify, assess, and control psychosocial hazards, which include any work-related factors that may cause psychological harm (Comcare, 2024). Claims for psychological injury at work are increasing at a rate that is far outstripping physical injury claims. In the Australian state of New South Wales, physical injury claims rose 11 per cent over the four years to mid-2023, while claims of psychological damage jumped 30 per cent over the same period (Rose and Thou, 2024).

As we have learned in previous chapters, neurodivergent individuals face unique challenges in the workplace compared to their neurotypical counterparts. Autistic employees, for instance, may experience heightened sensitivity to sensory inputs like bright lights or loud noises, leading to significant stress and anxiety. ADHD'ers can face difficulties with executive functioning skills such as time management, organisation, and sustaining attention on tasks. Also, autistic and ADHD individuals are more susceptible to mental health issues like anxiety and depression. As noted in Australia's Draft National Autism Strategy, autistic people are 2.5 times more likely to experience depression than the general population (Australian Government, 2024).

Whether through staff turnover, absenteeism, or long-term psychological injury which can lead to workers' compensation claims, the cost of inaction for employers is high. To support neurodivergent employees effectively, organisations need to adopt proactive and inclusive strategies at the team level and invest in equipping managers. Here are some key steps:

- **Provide training and awareness:** Educate employees about neurodivergence and the specific needs of neurodivergent individuals;

- **Measure who you employ and how they identify:** HR practitioners can help workplaces understand themselves, through data;

- **Conduct regular risk assessments:** Identify potential psychosocial hazards and implement measures to mitigate them;

- **Offer flexible work arrangements:** Allow flexible work hours or remote working options to help neurodivergent employees manage their workload in a way that suits their needs; and

- **Implement clear policies and procedures:** Develop policies that support neurodivergent employees, such as providing quiet spaces, allowing for sensory breaks, and offering mentorship (Mercer, 2024).

A meeting with a government minister provided an insight into the challenges of translating organisational commitments to diversity into teams.

The minister is on time!

The weeks that followed Xceptional winning the $1m Google Org Impact Challenge in 2018 can only be described as frantic. Our small social enterprise had been thrust into the spotlight, and frankly we were not prepared. News outlets, business leaders, and politicians all wanted our time. As a small business struggling to gain traction, we said yes to everything and later worked out how to accommodate each request.

Tuesday morning, we were due to meet a government minister who wanted to visit our office. I didn't have the heart to tell the minister's assistant that our office was the small corner of a co-working space. We hastily arranged for a meeting room and designed a pull-up banner to give the impression that the space was ours. The minister and his assistant arrived on time; they were easy to spot as they were the only people wearing suits in a building full of entrepreneurs wearing T-shirts.

The minister was generous with his time and curious about our work. We spent over an hour in our "office" discussing programmes to get diverse people into work and the role of governments in supporting social enterprise. The minister was a veteran of politics; he must have been in his mid-60s and projected a gentlemanly manner. However, the tone of the meeting and the minister's demeanour changed significantly when I asked why the government's disability

and refugee hiring initiatives were struggling to meet their
objectives. I was not trying to catch the minister out like
reporters do in press conferences. I was simply responding
to the minister's comments that it is hard work convincing
employers to hire diverse workers.

"I can't swear I front of the ladies", was the minister's response
when I asked for a second time why the programmes were
struggling. Finally, he blurted out, "Assholes". We each looked
around the room in surprise. He went on to explain that he
had several commitments from CEOs of large employers
who were happy to make a public commitment to hiring
diverse workers, and pose for a photo. I later discovered that
politicians love announcements and photo opportunities.
The minister's frustration was directed at hiring managers
who "only saw problems" and were "scared" when asked to
support the CEO's public pledge.

The challenge the minister faced in delivering two programmes
which aimed to grow labour force participation for people with
disabilities and refugees was similar to our struggle to gain traction in the investment bank. Simply put, there was a misalign-
ment between senior leaders who supported diversity with their
words and the actions of middle managers who failed to put
promise into action.

Organisations and senior leaders who pledge commitment to
diversity and inclusion, set quotas, and accept industry awards
rely on managers of small teams to make good on these commitments. In most cases, the CEOs and senior leaders have the
best of intentions. However, the success (or failure) of those good
intentions lies with the middle managers, many of whom are

under pressure on many fronts to deliver, feel under-resourced, and when they (at last!) have a new headcount approved may be reluctant to hire someone they are less confident they can manage effectively.

Middle managers play a critical role in culture change. They are central to the success or failure of change initiatives. Giangreco and Peccei (2005) argue that middle managers who resist change do so by failing to actively support change rather than openly opposing it. This research mirrors my experience, where the middle manager or team case for diversity is unclear, making it difficult to galvanise manager support.

One possibility for the lack of support for diversity and inclusion at the middle manager level is a failure to define the team case. Today's workplaces expect a lot from managers, and my experience is many are just hanging on under the pressure and extreme pace of work. I have learned to be patient and kind when dealing with middle managers as having walked in their shoes, I can appreciate the pressure they are under.

Conclusion

There is no shortage of evidence that diverse organisations, if supported by an inclusive culture and leadership, can hold a competitive advantage. The challenge in many workplaces is translating organisational wide commitments of diversity and inclusion to small operational teams. Diversity and inclusion can be hard to get right. Neuroinclusion offers tangible business benefits, from increased innovation to enhanced productivity, challenging the traditional charity-based view. To realise the benefits of neuroinclusion at a team level, managers need to understand the nature of their team, how they operate, what they believe, and what they are trying to achieve. Finally, the business case for investing in initiatives to attract and hire neurodivergent staff will depend on the type of team and what they are trying to accomplish. The case for investing in activities to support the inclusion of existing neurodivergent staff, such as neuroinclusion training and flexible working, can be made on moral and business grounds.

9
Conclusion

As we finish our time together, we return to the second meeting room, where nervous hiring managers and human resource business partners have finished watching the Melbourne Cup. While the conversations following our presentation were brief, the fears and questions raised that Tuesday afternoon have been repeated countless times in the years since. I wrote *Untapped Talent* to answer the questions that managers dare not ask in public. Questions that were whispered in that second room. These questions were born from fears of difference, ignorance, and political correctness.

Through a combination of lived experience, storytelling, and research I have provided managers and staff with a practical guide on inclusive recruitment, retainment, and advancement of neurodivergent people. Now that you have reached this point, it is your turn to turn this advice into practice. What advice would I leave with those gathered in the room? What tone would I use? Where would they start?

I would start by acknowledging that today's workplaces expect a lot from managers. Over the past few years, workplace leaders have navigated a global pandemic, rapid technological change, the great resignation, and the shifting expectations of Gen Z and Millennial workers. The weight on their shoulders is already knee-buckling heavy. My observation is that much of the commentary about inclusion for neurodivergent people is shouted at managers, not written with them. I would start by being a little kinder to managers, listening to their concerns and follow by dropping the word "should" from my vocabulary. Managers already have a lot of "should'" in their schedules.

From there I would use the following three simple steps that will cut through the noise of competing priorities, the fear of those in charge, and the posturing of the diversity, equity, and inclusion movement:

1. **Education.** First, I would suggest the managers chip away at their fear of the unknown by making neurodivergence a little less unknown. As we have discovered, education is key to reducing bias, countering stereotypes among neurotypicals, while making it safer and more relevant for neurodivergent employees to disclose if they wish. Remember, workplaces don't need to be led by experts, so if you are advising your organisation, be realistic and patient. There are an increasing number of resources available; depending on the market you operate in, there may be local experts who can assist.

As we covered in Chapter 5, whenever possible bring neurodivergent staff into the planning and learn from them and their lived expertise. They may not want to deliver training, but if you take time to listen, they can be your best teachers. It is likely that starting the conversation about neurodivergence in the workplace will lead to neurodivergent staff coming forward and disclosing. Each disclose creates an opportunity to listen to and learn from your staff.

Remember, everyone is different, and if you have met one neurodivergent person you have met one neurodivergent person. Refer to Chapter 5, where I provided an onboarding guide for introducing neurodivergent identity. I have reflected through writing this book whether I would have continued to keep my diagnosis hidden if past workplaces provided training. While I can't rewrite the past, I would likely have been open as I have seen hundreds of neurodivergent people be, following neuroinclusion training.

2. **Visibility.** Second, consider ways to measure who you already employ, and how they identify. Move beyond the standard ways of asking candidates to identify in the context of reasonable adjustments to a recruitment process. Rather, position any data capture by acknowledging that everyone thinks and works differently. As an inclusive employer you recognise the need to know more about how diverse minds function to ensure everyone can contribute to organisational success. If done properly, capturing data on how staff identify will help bust a large myth. Neurodivergence is not "out there", beyond your organisation. It is already here, you very likely have neurodivergent staff, customers, and stakeholders.

3. **Listen.** Finally, once you have started with education, seen evidence of the neurodivergent staff, customers, and stakeholders you already have, it's your opportunity to listen to them and act on their feedback. Depending on the size of your organisation, you could have neurodivergent people in a variety of positions, from senior leaders to graduates. Be prepared that some may not want to work with you to change your organisation, preferring

to get on with their jobs. There will be others who, as natural pattern detectives, incapable of sugar coating their message, can provide valuable insights. For example, I have witnessed neuro-divergent leaders who, through a combination of vulnerability and humour, have both led and actively participated in impor-tant conversations about workplace culture. Finally, there will be your willing coalition, who will embrace with you a desire for a more inclusive, more diverse workplace and will help you openly advocate for and reap the benefits of change!

Tipping point

The 2017 *Harvard Business Review* article, "Neurodiversity as a Competitive Advantage" (Austin and Pisano, 2017) was the start of an awakening. Evidence can be drawn from the volume of aca-demic writing on the subject of "Neurodiversity in the Workplace". Searching the Griffith University Library online, which my indus-try fellowship afforded me, I found 20 articles in total prior to 2017. Since 2018, the number of articles is 292, of which 250 have been authored since 2021. These academic writings, when com-bined with increased media representation, point to a growing awareness of neurodiversity in the last few years.

It can be common that change is not felt evenly. Indeed, pro-gress has varied across different regions. From my observations, Northern Europe, the United Kingdom, and Ireland, along with the United States and Canada, are leading the way. Progress in my home market of Australia has been slower. While there are some notable programmes covered throughout this book, most employers are still on the starting blocks. Counter to the global perception of Australians as laid-back people, our business culture is both conservative and risk adverse. Historically, efforts to include neurodivergent people into the workforce have been tied to a crowded diversity, equity, and inclusion agenda rather than the business imperatives covered in Chapter 8. It may take several years for markets like Australia to learn from and contextualise lessons from neuroinclusion leaders, and this amounts to missed opportunities for employers.

I would like to conclude our time with one of my favourite examples of workplace inclusion. A market-leading AI employer in South Korea has adopted an innovative and inclusive approach to attracting and retaining talent, with impressive results.

Solving tomorrow's challenges

At 32, Lee has finally found his place. Growing up in a middle-class district of Seoul, Lee was diagnosed with autism in high school, and later, with anxiety. Lee, excelled at school, showing promise in art, computer science, and mathematics. His first job in data entry was stressful and ended abruptly for reasons Lee still doesn't understand. This is not unusual; I have spoken with dozens of neurodivergent people who have been let go for vague reasons, often resulting in months of stressful rumination and self-blame over what might have gone wrong.

Today, Lee is working with a leading AI company, performing the important task of data annotation, which entails accurate categorisation and labelling of images. The training data produced by Lee and his colleagues supports self-driving vehicle programs for global manufacturers and technology companies. Now in his third year, Lee is thriving, sharing "unlike my previous job, it's not stressful. The working environment is better than my previous job, and I am treated with respect". Lee goes on to describe the connections he has made with colleagues and the kindness of managers and support staff.

Lee's colleagues describe him as punctual, quirky, and meticulous. One quirky behaviour is Lee's love of imitating public transportation announcements whenever he provides instructions to colleagues. Lee imagines himself as the driver and his colleagues as passengers. Lee says he "strives for perfection in his work and feels insecure if it is not done thoroughly". This perfection is called for as the accuracy and safety of AI programs for self-driving cars are literally a matter of life or death. Both the company and those dependent on self-driving technology benefit from Lee's skills and efforts. Lee has been recognised for his work with an annual performance reward, the company noting his error rate is 20 per cent lower than his peers.

To attract and retain talented people like Lee, the South Korean employer adopted an alternative approach. First, the formal interview was scrapped, in exchange for a paid three-day work trial. A tailored onboarding and support structure was adopted, while managers are encouraged to provide continuous feedback. Task allocation and project management now includes detailed workflows, which all staff benefit from. The company has refined its approach over the past five years and is now a leader in this growing field.

Companies and governments solving our most pressing challenges, such as climate change, next generation transport, or anticipating the next pandemic, need all kinds of minds. We need more people like Lee.

Managers, it is your turn

Neuroinclusion calls on workplaces and managers to adopt an approach that sounds simple but will require additional effort. The approach calls for a person-centred focus where staff are placed in an inclusive environment that maximises their contributions. Technology giant SAP use a metaphor to communicate this concept. "People are like puzzle pieces, irregularly shaped. Historically, companies have asked employees to trim away their irregularities, because it's easier to for people together if they are all perfect rectangles. But that requires employees to leave their differences at home, differences firms need to innovate. To embrace this approach requires "managers to do the hard work of fitting irregular puzzle pieces together, to treat people not as containers of fungible human resources but as unique individual assets. The work for managers will be harder, but the payoff for companies will be considerable" (Austin and Pisano 2017, p. 103). While I acknowledge the opposition from the neurodivergent community with the notion that we are puzzles to be solved, I believe our uniqueness is a strength that employers need to adjust to, not the other way around.

There is not scope in this book to fully unpack what support and resources are available for managers, who will shoulder a lot of the work required to fully include neurodivergent employees into the workplace. For now, it is important to acknowledge that challenge, and be prepared to be patient and kind if you find yourself spearheading an initiative.

Neurodivergent people are not scary, we just think a little differently, and may come across like Lee as a little quirky. Some may come across as a lot quirky for that matter, and that is ok. Ask yourself, would you put up with train announcements in team meetings in exchange for 20 per cent reduction in errors? It may not be that simple, but an approach grounded in humble curiosity and open-mindedness that seeks to first ask the person before assuming will be a welcome start.

Neuroinclusion is a rapidly evolving, nuanced, and still widely untapped domain. To stay across the latest, I have included resources at the end of this chapter. Once again, you don't need to be an expert, but a little knowledge goes a long way.

My experience, what worked and what didn't

"Having never thought of writing a book I didn't know where to start" (email sent to Dr Damian Mellifont, Lived Experience Postdoctoral Fellow, 31 January 2023). And so began my 18-month experiment to write this book. I have never been great at thanking people, it's not that I am ungrateful, it is more likely I have moved onto the next thing and failed to stop to appreciate the support. Writing affords me the opportunity to slow down now and be thankful.

I would like to start by thanking the Lived Places Publishing, Disabilities Studies Collection Editors, Dr Damian Mellifont and Professor Jennifer Smith-Merry. My thanks also goes to the Co-Founder and Publisher of Lived Places Publishing, David Parker, for providing an opportunity for diverse stories to be told.

Untapped Talent, while not a formal research thesis, is rather a collection of my personal and professional experiences along with insights drawn from many years of conversations. You will have noted that to protect the identity of subjects I have changed the names throughout. To the business leaders, managers, and allies who shared your views on neuroinclusion, you know who you are, thank you. To the neurodivergent people themselves, many of whom revisited past workplace trauma, thank you for your bravery and honesty. It has been a joy and honour to meet with people from around the world, all working to the same end. Finally, to my family, who made space for my deep work, and accommodated my grumpy face. I love you.

For any aspiring neurodivergent authors out there, I can share that some aspects of writing, such as drafting stories, contacting people from around the world, and asking for help required little effort. It helped to have a regular time to write, for me this usually started at 5.30 a.m. before my work day officially started. I was also aided with time management by setting app limits on my phone and having clear goals of delivering a chapter every four to six weeks. Finally, using the anchor of Garry Cattermole's employee lifecycle was helpful in focusing my attention at each stage.

What didn't work is stopping writing when work and family commitments became overwhelming. I had to push out two deadlines, which for someone who is always on time was stressful. In hindsight it would have been better to stick with it, even writing a small amount each week, as the time taken to get back into the flow was more than I anticipated. Through *Untapped Talent*, I have attempted to blend real-word examples, lived experience, and academic research which felt clunky to me at times. My ADHD makes reading research, particularly the punctuation, very hard as I find the authors and years of publication a distraction. I know I am not alone in this. Add in brain fog, procrastination, and rabbit holes of research, and I am grateful to be at the end.

Further reading

While my work in neuroinclusion continues, yours may just be starting. Thank you for taking the time to read *Untapped Talent*. If you have any feedback, questions, or suggestions, you can reach me at http://aronmercer.com.

Finally, below is a list of suggested resources with weblinks for further reading.

- **Stanford Neurodiversity Project** – This project, part of Stanford Medicine, provides resources and support for creating neurodiverse-friendly workplaces. They offer programmes and initiatives to help employers understand and leverage neurodiverse talent. https://med.stanford.edu/neurodiversity.html

- **auticon** – auticon is an IT consulting business that employs autistic adults as IT consultants. They provide neurodiversity training and consultancy services to help organisations become more inclusive. Their approach focuses on leveraging the unique strengths of autistic individuals in the workplace. https://auticon.com/

- **Mentra** – Mentra is a neurodiverse employment network that connects neurodivergent individuals with inclusive employers. They provide resources and tools for creating inclusive hiring practices and supporting neurodivergent employees in the workplace. https://www.mentra.com/

- **DisabilityIN** – DisabilityIN is a nonprofit resource for business disability inclusion worldwide. They provide tools, resources, and training to help organisations build inclusive workplaces for people with disabilities, including those who are neurodivergent. https://disabilityin.org/

- **The Valuable 500** – The Valuable 500 is a global movement putting disability on the business leadership agenda. They work with CEOs and their companies to drive systemic change and unlock the business, social, and economic value of the 1.3 billion people living with disabilities around the world, including neurodivergent individuals. https://www.thevaluable500.com/

- **Neurodiversity Hub** – Neurodiversity Hub provides resources for employers to create neurodiverse-friendly workplaces. They offer guidance on inclusive hiring practices, workplace accommodations, and support for neurodivergent employees. https://www.neurodiversityhub.org/

- **Genius Within** – Genius Within is an organisation that supports neurodivergent individuals in the workplace by providing coaching, training, and assessments. They help employers create inclusive environments that leverage the strengths of neurodivergent employees. https://geniuswithin.org/

- **DXC Dandelion Program** – The DXC Dandelion Program focuses on creating sustainable employment opportunities for neurodivergent individuals in the technology sector. They provide training, coaching, and support to help organisations integrate neurodivergent talent successfully. https://dxc.com/au/en/about-us/social-impact-practice/dxc-dandelion-program

- **Ultranauts** – Ultranauts is a quality engineering firm that taps into the talents of neurodivergent individuals, particularly those on the autism spectrum. They provide training, coaching, and inclusive employment opportunities to help organisations improve quality and efficiency. https://ultranauts.co/company/

- **Deloitte** – Deloitte provides insights and strategies for creating a neuroinclusive workplace, offering resources to help organisations leverage the talents of neurodivergent employees and create an inclusive environment. https://www.deloitte.com/global/en/about/people/social-responsibility/neurodiversity-at-deloitte.html

Suggested discussion topics

Following are some questions to prompt critical discussion:

- What are the barriers to disclosing neurodivergence in the workplace and how might these be redressed?
- What are some of the key barriers and enablers to recruiting neurodivergent employees?
- In what evidence-based ways can employers support the retainment of neurodivergent employees?
- How can more neurodivergent employees be supported to reach leadership positions?
- What are some of benefits of employing neurodivergent employees?

References

Accardo, A. L., Pontes, N. M. H., and Pontes, M. C. F. (2022. Heightened Anxiety and Depression Among Autistic Adolescents with ADHD: Findings from the National Survey of Children's Health 2016–2019. *Journal of Autism and Developmental Disorders*, 54(2), pp. 563–576. https://doi.org/10.1007/s10803-022-05803-9

ADA.gov. (2024). The Americans with Disabilities Act. U.S. Department of Justice. [Online] Available at: www.ada.gov/ [Accessed 28 July 2024].

ADDitude. (2023). Famous people with ADHD. *ADDitude*. [Online] Available at: www.additudemag.com/slideshows/famous-people-with-adhd/

ADHD Australia. (2024). About ADHD. [Online] *ADHD Australia*. Available at: www.adhdaustralia.org.au/about-adhd/

Adler, P. & Kwon, S,W. (2002). Social Capital: Prospects for A New Concept. Academy of Management Review. 27. 17-40. 10.5465/AMR.2002.5922314.

AHRI. (2023). AHRI Report. Australian HR Institute. [Online] Available at: www.ahri.com.au/wp-content/uploads/AHRI-report_15.5.23.pdf [Accessed 28 July 2024].

Alonzo, J. (2023). Focusing on the high cost of employee turnover. [Online] Randstad Australia. Available at: www.randstad.com.au/hr-news/attracting-recruiting-talent/focusing-high-cost-employee-turnover/ [Accessed 28 July 2024].

Annabi, H., Crooks, E. W., Barnett, N., Guadagno, J., Mahoney, J. R., Michelle, J., Pacilio, A., Shukla, H. and Velasco, J. (2021). *Autism @ Work Playbook: Finding Talent and Creating Meaningful Employment Opportunities for People with Aautism*. 2nd ed.

Seattle, WA: ACCESS-IT, The Information School, University of Washington.

Anonymous. (2017). What I wish I could tell my boss: "My autism is not a problem." *Guardian*. [Online] Available at: www.theguard ian.com/careers/2017/jul/07/what-i-wish-i-could-tell-my-boss-my-autism-is-not-a-problem

Austin, R. and Pisano, G. (2017). Neurodiversity as a competitive advantage. [Online] Available at: https://hbr.org/2017/05/neu rodiversity-as-a-competitive-advantage

Australian Government. (2024). Draft National Autism Strategy. https://engage.dss.gov.au/wp-content/uploads/2024/05/draft-national-autism-strategy-003.pdf

Bell, S. T., Villado, A. J., Lukasik, M. A., Belau, L. and Briggs, A. L. (2011). Getting Specific about Demographic Diversity Variable and Team Performance Relationships: A Meta-analysis. *Journal of Management*, 37(3), pp. 709–743. https://doi.org/10.1177/01492 06310365001

Biggs, J. (2024). Celebrities with Autism: From Tallulah Willis to Elon Musk, Meet the Famous Faces on the Autistic Spectrum. *Cosmopolitan*. [Online] Available at: www.cosmopolitan.com/uk/body/health/g44048763/celebrities-with-autism/ [Accessed 5 August 2024].

Bika, N. (2022). The most common recruiting challenges and how to overcome them. 26 May. [Online] Available at: https://resour ces.workable.com/stories-and-insights/common-recruiting-cha llenges

Bilton, N. (2009). Part of the daily American diet, 34 gigabytes of gata. *The New York Times*. [Online] Available at: www.nytimes.com/2009/12/10/technology/10data.html [Accessed 3 August 2024].

Blume, H. (1998). Neurodiversity: On the neurological underpin- nings of geekdom. *The Atlantic*, September. [Online] Available at: www.theatlantic.com/magazine/archive/1998/09/neurodi versity/305909/ [Accessed 12 August 2024].

Bourke, J. and Dillon, B. (2018). The diversity and inclusion revolution. Eight powerful truths. *Deloitte Review*, 22, January.

Brassey, J., Coe, E., Dewhurst, M., Enomoto, K., Giarola, R., Herbig, B. and Jeffery, B., 2022. Addressing employee burnout: Are you solving the right problem? *McKinsey Health Institute*. Available at: https://www.mckinsey.com/mhi/our-insights/addressing-employee-burnout-are-you-solving-the-right-problem [Accessed 28 July 2024]

Brown, L. (2021). Vice Admiral Nick Hine: To be blunt: Autism made me a better naval officer. *The Times*. [Online] Available at: www.thetimes.com/uk/politics/article/vice-admiral-nick-hine-to-be-blunt-autism-made-me-a-better-naval-officer-rvg8p8rxl [Accessed 28 July 2024].

Cappadocia, M. C., Weiss, J. A. and Pepler, D. (2012). Bullying Experiences among Children and Youth with Autism Spectrum Disorders. *Journal of Autism and Developmental Disorders*, 42(2), pp. 266–277. https://doi.org/10.1007/s10803-011-1241-x. Available at: https://pubmed.ncbi.nlm.nih.gov/21499672/ [Accessed 3 August 2024].

Carnahan, B. and Moore, C. (2023). Actively addressing unconscious bias in recruiting. [Online] Harvard Business School. Available at: www.hbs.edu/recruiting/insights-and-advice/blog/post/actively-addressing-unconscious-bias-in-recruiting [Accessed 2 August 2024].

Castilla, Emilio J. and Ranganathan, A. (2020). "The Production of Merit: How Managers Understand and Apply Merit in the Workplace." *Organization Science*, 31(4), pp. 909–35. https://doi.org/10.1287/orsc.2019.1335.

Cattermole, G. (2019). Developing the Employee Lifecycle to Keep Top Talent. *Strategic HR Review*, 18(6), pp. 258–262.

Chanland, D. E. and Murphy, W. M. (2018). Propelling Diverse Leaders to the Top: A Developmental Network Approach. *Human Resource Management*, 57(1), pp. 111–126.

Chodavadia, P., Teo, I., Poremski, D., Fung, D. S. S. and Finkelstein, E. A. (2023). Prevalence and Economic Burden of Depression and Anxiety Symptoms among Singaporean Adults: Results from a 2022 Web Panel. *BMC Psychiatry*, 23(1), p. 104. https://doi.org/10.1186/s12888-023-04581-7

Chong, D. and Druckman, J. N. (2007). Framing Theory. *Annual Review of Political Science*, 10, pp. 103–126. https://doi.org/10.1146/annurev.polisci.10.072805.103054

Cleveland Clinic. (2024). Rejection Sensitive Dysphoria (RSD): Symptoms & treatment. [Online] Cleveland Clinic. Available at: https://my.clevelandclinic.org/health/diseases/24099-rejection-sensitive-dysphoria-rsd [Accessed 28 July 2024].

Collins Dictionary. (2024). Inclusive of. [Online] Collins English Dictionary. Available at: www.collinsdictionary.com/dictionary/english/inclusive-of

Comcare. (2024). Changes to WHS laws. [Online] Comcare. Available at: www.comcare.gov.au/safe-healthy-work/prevent-harm/changes-to-whs-laws [Accessed 28 July 2024].

Connell, L. (2019) What have labels ever done for us? The linguistic shortcut in conceptual processing, Language, Cognition and Neuroscience, 34:10, 1308–1318, DOI: 10.1080/23273798.2018.1471512

Culture Amp. (2024). Neurodiversity in the workplace: Why it matters. [Online] Culture Amp. Available at: www.cultureamp.com/blog/neurodiversity-in-the-workplace

Davies, J., Heasman, B., Livesey, A., Walker, A., Pellicano, E. and Remington, A. (2023). Access to Employment: A Comparison of Autistic, Neurodivergent and Neurotypical Adults' Experiences of Hiring Processes in the United Kingdom. *Autism*, 27(6), pp. 1746–1763.

Department of Social Services. (2024). Draft National Autism Strategy. [Online] Department of Social Services. Available at: https://engage.dss.gov.au/wp-content/uploads/2024/05/draft-national-autism-strategy-003.pdf

DeSantis, M., 2023. Celebrities with dyslexia, ADHD, and dyscalculia. [Online] *Understood*. Available at: www.understood.org/en/articles/success-stories-celebrities-with-dyslexia-adhd-and-dyscalculia [Accessed 5 August 2024].

Diversity Council Australia, 2023. Inclusive language. *Diversity Council Australia*. Available at: https://www.dca.org.au/resources/di-planning/inclusive-language [Accessed 28 July 2024]

Dixon-Fyle, S., Dolan, K., Hunt, V. and Prince, S. (2020). Diversity wins: How inclusion matters. [Online] McKinsey & Company. Available at: www.mckinsey.com/featured-insights/diversity-and-inclusion/diversity-wins-how-inclusion-matters [Accessed 2 August 2024].

Dodson, W. (2020). Rejection Sensitive Dysphoria (RSD): ADHD and emotional dysregulation. *ADDitude Magazine*. [Online] Available at: www.additudemag.com/rejection-sensitive-dysphoria-adhd/ [Accessed 28 July 2024].

Doyle, N. (2020). Neurodiversity at Work: A Biopsychosocial Model and the Impact on Working Adults. *British Medical Bulletin.*, 14 October, 135(1), pp.108–125. doi: 10.1093/bmb/ldaa021. PMID: 32996572; PMCID: PMC7732033. [Accessed 14 August 2024].

DXC Technology. (2023). Social impact practice year in review 2023. [Online] Available at: https://dxc.com/content/dam/dxc/projects/dxc-com/au/About%20Us/social-impact-practice/pdfs/dxc-au-social-impact-practice-year-in-review-2023.pdf [Accessed 28 July 2024].

Edith Cowan University. (2023). Inclusive language at work. Edith Cowan University. [Online] Available at: https://studyonline.ecu.edu.au/blog/inclusive-language-work

Edmondson, A. (1999). Psychological Safety and Learning Behavior in Work Teams. *Administrative Science Quarterly*, 44(2), pp. 350–383.

Ernst & Young. (2024). Quality management system auditor. [Online] EY Careers. Available at: https://careers.ey.com/ey/job/Sydney-Quality-Management-System-Auditor-NSW-NSW-2000/1080483301/ [Accessed 2 August 2024].

Federal Register of Legislation. (2023). Disability Discrimination Act 1992. [Online] Federal Register of Legislation. Available at: www.legislation.gov.au/C2004A04426/latest/text [Accessed 28 July 2024].

Fevre, R., Robinson, A., Lewis, D. and Jones, T. (2013). The Ill-treatment of Employees with Disabilities in British Workplaces. *Work, Employment and Society*, 27(2), pp. 288–307.

Forret, M. F. and Dougherty, T. W. (2004). Networking Behavior and Career Outcomes: Differences for Men and Women. *Journal of Organizational Behavior*, 25(3), pp. 419–437.

Frieder, R. E., Van Iddekinge, C. H. and Raymark, P. H. (2015). How Quickly Do Interviewers Reach Decisions? An Examination of Interviewers' Decision-making Time across Applicants. *Journal of Occupational and Organizational Psychology*, 89(2), pp. 223–248. https://doi.org/10.1111/joop.12118

George Washington University, 2020. Equity vs. Equality: What's the difference? *George Washington University Online Public Health*. Available at: https://onlinepublichealth.gwu.edu/resources/equity-vs-equality/

Giangreco, A. and Peccei, R. (2005). The Nature and Antecedents of Middle Manager Resistance to Change: Evidence from an Italian Context. *The International Journal of Human Resource Management*, 16(10), pp. 1812–1829. https://doi.org/10.1080/09585190500298404

Goering, S. (2015). Rethinking Disability: The Social Model of Disability and Chronic Disease. *Current Review of Musculoskeletal Medicine*, 8(2), pp. 134–138. https://doi.org/10.1007/s12 178-015-9273-z

Goler, L., Gale, J., Harrington, B. and Grant, A. (2018). Why people really quit their jobs. *Harvard Business Review*. [Online] Available at: https://hbr.org/2018/01/why-people-really-quit-their-jobs [Accessed 28 July 2024].

Gov.uk. (2024). Equality Act 2010: guidance. [Online] Gov.uk. Available at: www.gov.uk/guidance/equality-act-2010-guida nce#overview [Accessed 28 July 2024].

Griffiths, C., 2024. 10 highly successful people you didn't know were neurodivergent. *CEO Today*. [Online] Available at: www.ceoto daymagazine.com/2024/06/10-highly-successful-people-you-didnt-know-were-neurodivergent/ [Accessed 5 August 2024].

Hallowell, E. and Ratey, J. (2024). ADHD needs a better name. We have one. *ADDitude Magazine*. [Online] Available at: www.addi tudemag.com/attention-deficit-disorder-vast/

Henneborn, L. (2021). Make it safe for employees to disclose their disabilities. *Harvard Business Review*. [Online] Available at: https:// hbr.org/2021/06/make-it-safe-for-employees-to-disclose-their-disabilities

Herring, C. (2009). Does Diversity Pay? Race, Gender, and the Business Case for Diversity. *American Sociological Review*, 74(April), pp. 208–224.

• Hogan, A. J. (2019). Social and Medical Models of Disability and Mental Health: Evolution and Renewal. Canadian Medical Association Journal, 191(1), pp. E16–E18. https://doi.org/10.1503/ cmaj.181008

Hoover DW, Kaufman J. Adverse childhood experiences in children with autism spectrum disorder. Curr Opin Psychiatry.

2018 Mar;31(2):128–132. doi: 10.1097/YCO.0000000000000390. PMID: 29206686; PMCID: PMC6082373.

Hours C, Recasens C and Baleyte J-M (2022) ASD and ADHD Comorbidity: What Are We Talking About? Front. Psychiatry 13:837424. doi: 10.3389/fpsyt.2022.837424

Hull L, Petrides KV, Allison C, Smith P, Baron-Cohen S, Lai MC, Mandy W. "Putting on My Best Normal": Social Camouflaging in Adults with Autism Spectrum Conditions. J Autism Dev Disord. 2017 Aug;47(8):2519–2534. doi: 10.1007/s10803-017-3166-5. PMID: 28527095; PMCID: PMC5509825.

Hunkenschroer, A. and Lütge, C. (2022). Ethics of AI-Enabled Recruiting and Selection: A Review and Research Agenda. *Journal of Business Ethics*, 178. https://doi.org/10.1007/s10 551-022-05049-6

IMDb. (2024). *Up in the Air* (2009) – George Clooney as Ryan Bingham. [Online] IMDb. Available at: www.imdb.com/title/ tt1193138/characters/nm0000123 [Accessed 28 July 2024].

Javetski, B. and Koller, T. (2018). Debiasing the corporation: An interview with Nobel laureate Richard Thaler. *McKinsey Quarterly*. [Online] Available at: www.mckinsey.com/capabilities/strategy- and-corporate-finance/our-insights/debiasing-the-corporation- an-interview-with-nobel-laureate-richard-thaler. [Accessed 28 July 2024].

Johns ML.2013. Breaking the glass ceiling: structural, cul- tural, and organizational barriers preventing women from achieving senior and executive positions. Perspect Health Inf Manag. 2013;10(Winter):1e. Epub 2013 Jan 1. PMID: 23346029; PMCID: PMC3544145.

JPMorgan Chase, 2023. Proven value: Autism at work. *JPMorgan Chase Newsroom*. Available at: https://www.jpmorganchase. com/newsroom/stories/autism-at-work [Accessed 28 July 2024].

Kash, N., 2021. How to ace your job interview: An ADHD primer. *ADDitude Magazine.* Available at: https://www.additudemag. com/job-interview-tips-adhd-primer/ [Accessed 28 July 2024].

Keller, H. (1926). *My Key of Life.* New York: Doubleday, Page & Company, p. 38. Available at: https://archive.org/details/myke yoflife0000hele/page/38/mode/2up [Accessed 2 August 2024].

Key AP, D'Ambrose Slaboch K. 2021. Speech Processing in Autism Spectrum Disorder: An Integrative Review of Auditory Neurophysiology Findings. J Speech Lang Hear Res. 2021 Nov 8;64(11):4192–4212. doi: 10.1044/2021_JSLHR-20-00738. Epub 2021 Sep 27. PMID: 34570613; PMCID: PMC9132155.

Kirby, A. (2021). Is There a Link Between Neurodiversity and Mental Health? *Psychology Today.* [Online] Available at: www.psyc hologytoday.com/au/blog/pathways-progress/202108/is-there-link-between-neurodiversity-and-mental-health [Accessed 3 August 2024].

Limburg, J., 2019. Is my autism a superpower? *The Guardian.* [Online] Available at: www.theguardian.com/society/2019/nov/ 03/is-autism-a-superpower-greta-thunberg-and-others-think-it-can-be [Accessed 17 August 2024].

LSE. (2022) The London School of Economics and Political Science, Inclusive Leadership Through Behavioural Science, Module 6.

Maenner, M. J., Warren, Z., Williams, A. R., et al. (2023). Prevalence and Characteristics of Autism Spectrum Disorder Among Children Aged 8 Years – Autism and Developmental Disabilities Monitoring Network, 11 Sites, United States, 2020. *MMWR Surveillance Summaries,* 72(SS-2), pp. 1–14. http://dx.doi.org/ 10.15585/mmwr.ss7202a1.

Mahto, M., Sniderman, B. and Hogan, S. K. (2022). Neurodiversity in the workplace. Deloitte Insights. [Online] Available at: www2. deloitte.com/us/en/insights/topics/talent/neurodiversity-in-the-workplace.html [Accessed 28 July 2024].

Markel K. S., Elia B. (2016). How human resource management can best support employees with autism: Future directions for research and practice. *Journal of Business and Management*, 22(1), 71–85.

Marshall, C. (2024). The unbearable heartache of Rejection Sensitive Dysphoria. [Online] Reframing Autism. Available at: https://reframingautism.org.au/the-unbearable-heartache-of-rejection-sensitive-dysphoria/ [Accessed 28 July 2024].

Martins, L. L. (2020). Strategic Diversity Leadership: The Role of Senior Leaders in Delivering the Diversity Dividend. *Journal of Management*, 46(7), pp. 1191–1204.

McFeely, S. and Wigert, B. (2019). This fixable problem costs U.S. businesses $1 trillion. [Online] Gallup. Available at: www.gallup.com/workplace/247391/fixable-problem-costs-businesses-trillion.aspx [Accessed 28 July 2024].

McGinty, E. E., Stone, E. M., Kennedy-Hendricks, A. and Barry, C. L. (2019). Stigmatizing Language in News Media Coverage of the Opioid Epidemic: Implications for Public Health. *Preventive Medicine*, 124, pp. 110–114. https://doi.org/10.1016/j.ypmed.2019.03.018

McLean, K. J., Eack, S. M. and Bishop, L. (2021). The Impact of Sleep Quality on Quality of Life for Autistic Adults. *Research in Autism Spectrum Disorders*, 88, 101849. https://doi.org/10.1016/j.rasd.2021.101849. Epub 2021 Sep 1. PMID: 34539812; PMCID: PMC8442542.

Mellifont, D. (2021). Facilitators and Inhibitors of Mental Discrimination in the Workplace: A Traditional Review. *Studies in Social Justice*, 15(1), pp. 59–80.

Mensik, H. (2024). How companies like Microsoft, EY and Bank of America are hiring more neurodiverse staff. [Online] WorkLife. Available at: www.worklife.news/talent/neurodiversity-autism-adhd-hiring-interview-microsoft-ey/ [Accessed 28 July 2024].

Mercer, A. (2020). How to land your first job without having an interview. [Online] Xceptional. Available at: https://xceptional.io/employees/land-first-job-without-interview/

Mercer, A. (2024). Creating safe spaces: Addressing psychological safety in the workplace. [Online] Xceptional Academy. Available at: https://xceptionalacademy.org.au/2024/07/09/creating-safe-spaces-addressing-psychological-safety-in-the-workplace/ [Accessed 28 July 2024].

Miller, D., Rees, J. and Pearson, A. (2021). "Masking Is Life": Experiences of Masking in Autistic and Nonautistic Adults. *Autism in Adulthood*, 3(4), pp. 330–338. https://doi.org/10.1089/aut.2020.0083. Epub 2021 Dec 7. PMID: 36601640; PMCID: PMC8992921.

Moore, D. (2012). Stop being deceived by interviews when you're hiring. [Online] Forbes. Available at: www.forbes.com/sites/forbesleadershipforum/2012/02/07/stop-being-deceived-by-interviews-when-youre-hiring/?sh=386b87fa1bf6 [Accessed 2 August 2024].

Mortensen, Mark, and Amy C. Edmondson. "Rethink Your Employee Value Proposition: Offer Your People More Than Just Flexibility." Harvard Business Review 101, no. 1 (January–February 2023): 45–49.

National Institutes of Health (US) (2007). Information about the brain. Biological sciences curriculum study. NIH Curriculum Supplement Series. Bethesda (MD): National Institutes of Health (US). [Online] Available from: www.ncbi.nlm.nih.gov/books/NBK20367/

Nee, J., Macfarlane Smith, G., Rustagi, I., McElhaney, K. and Quasthof, L. (2023). *Understanding Inclusive Leadership: A Playbook*. Haas School of Business, University of California, Berkeley. [Online] Available at: https://haas.berkeley.edu/wp-content/uploads/Understanding-IL-Playbook-3.pdf

Nikolaou, Ioannis. (2021). What is the Role of Technology in Recruitment and Selection?. The Spanish Journal of Psychology. 24. 10.1017/SJP.2021.6.

O'Kane, C. (2021). Elon Musk reveals he has Asperger's during "Saturday Night Live" monologue. [Online] CBS News. Available at: www.cbsnews.com/news/elon-musk-aspergers-saturday-night-live/ [Accessed 28 July 2024].

O'Neil, C. (2016). *Weapons of Math Destruction: How Big Data Increases Inequality and Threatens Democracy*. Crown Publishing Group. United States of America

Omoigui, N., 2022. Workspaces failing needs of neurodiverse employees. *HR Magazine*. Available at: https://www.hrmagazine. co.uk/content/news/workspaces-failing-needs-of-neurodiverse-employees/ [Accessed 28 July 2024]

Petrolini, V., Jorba, M. and Vicente, A. (2023). What Does it Take to be Rigid? Reflections on the Notion of Rigidity in Autism. *Frontiers in Psychiatry*, 14, 1072362. https://doi.org/10.3389/fpsyt.2023.1072362. PMID: 36860504; PMCID: PMC9969081.

Polli, F. (2019). Using AI to eliminate bias from hiring. *Harvard Business Review*. [Online] Available at: https://hbr.org/2019/10/using-ai-to-eliminate-bias-from-hiring.

Popelka, J. (2022). *Experience, Inc.: Why Companies that Uncover Purpose, Create Connection, and Celebrate Their People Will Triumph*. Wiley. Available at: www.wiley.com/en-United States of America au/Experience%2C+Inc.%3A+Why+Companies+That+Uncover+Purpose%2C+Create+Connection%2C+and+Celebrate+Their+People+Will+Triumph-p-9781119852889 [Accessed 28 July 2024].

Powell, A. (2002). Improving Workforce Development. *Industrial and Commercial Training*, 34(5), pp. 176–181.

Praslova, L. N. (2024). *The Canary Code: A Guide to Neurodiversity, Dignity, and Intersectional Belonging at Work*. 1st ed. Berrett-Koehler Publishers, Inc. United States of America

Raymaker, D., 2022. Understanding autistic burnout. *National Autistic Society*. Available at: https://www.autism.org.uk/advice-and-guidance/professional-practice/autistic-burnout [Accessed 28 July 2024].

Rivera, L. A. (2012). Diversity within Reach: Recruitment versus Hiring in Elite Firms. *Annals of the American Academy of Political and Social Science*, 639, pp. 71–90.

Romualdez, Anna & Walker, Zachary & Remington, Anna. (2021). Autistic adults' experiences of diagnostic disclosure in the workplace: Decision-making and factors associated with outcomes. Autism & Developmental Language Impairments. 6. 239694152110229. 10.1177/23969415211022955.

Rose, T. and Thou, S. (2024). Claims for psychological injury at work surge in NSW at triple the rate of physical harm. The Guardian. [Online] Available at: www.theguardian.com/australia-news/article/2024/may/22/psychological-injury-claims-safework-nsw-rise-mental-health-statistics#:~:text=Physical%20injury%20claims%20rose%2011,the%20State%20Insurance%20Regulatory%20Authority [Accessed 28 July 2024].

Santuzzi, A. M., Martinez, J. J. and Keating, R. T. (2022). The Benefits of Inclusion for Disability Measurement in the Workplace. *Equality, Diversity and Inclusion: An International Journal*, 41(3), pp. 474–490.

Schwantes, M. (2018). Sir Richard Branson calls dyslexia a blessing in disguise, urges leaders to hire dyslexic professionals. [Online] Inc Australia. Available at: www.inc-aus.com/marcel-schwantes/sir-richard-branson-calls-dyslexia-a-blessing-in-disguise-urges-leaders-to-hire-dyslexic-professionals.html [Accessed 28 July 2024].

Sherbin, L., Kennedy, J. T., Jain-Link, P. and Ihezie, K. (2017). *Disabilities and Inclusion, US Findings*. Centre for Talent Innovation.

Smith, T. (2024). Neurodiversity with Theo Smith. [Online] Available at: https://podcasts.apple.com/pk/podcast/neurodi versity-with-theo-smith/id1480239272

Smith, T. and Kirby, A. (2021). *Neurodiversity at Work: Drive Innovation, Performance and Productivity with a Neurodiverse Workforce*. Kogan Page. United Kingdom.

Snyder, L. A., Carmichael, J. S., Blackwell, L. V., Cleveland, J. N. and Thornton, G. C. (2010). Perceptions of Discrimination and Justice among Employees with Disabilities. *Employee Responsibilities and Rights Journal*, 22, pp. 5–19.

Sull, D., Sull, C. and Zweig, B. (2022). Toxic culture is driving the Great Resignation. *MIT Sloan Management Review*. [Online] Available at: https://sloanreview.mit.edu/article/toxic-culture-is-driving-the-great-resignation/ [Accessed 28 July 2024].

Trivella, C., 2023. What culture add means to organizational growth and why it is so important now. *Forbes Human Resources Council*. Available at: https://www.forbes.com/sites/forbeshu manresourcescouncil/2023/05/05/what-culture-add-means-to-organizational-growth-and-why-it-is-so-important-now/

University of California, San Francisco (2024). Unconscious Bias Training. [Online] UCSF Office of Diversity and Outreach. Available at: https://diversity.ucsf.edu/programs-resources/training/unco nscious-bias-training [Accessed 28 July 2024].

University of Melbourne. (2012). Self-confidence the secret to workplace advancement. *ScienceDaily*. [Online] Available at: www.sciencedaily.com/releases/2012/10/121018103214.htm [Accessed 28 July 2024].

Von Schrader, S., Malzer, V. & Bruyère, S. (2014) Perspectives on Disability Disclosure: The Importance of Employer Practices and

Workplace Climate. *Employ Respons Rights J* 26, 237–255. https://doi.org/10.1007/s10672-013-9227-9

Wagner, R. K., Zirps, F. A., Edwards, A. A., Wood, S. G., Joyner, R. E., Becker, B. J., Liu, G. and Beal, B. (2020). The Prevalence of Dyslexia: A New Approach to Its Estimation. *Journal of Learning Disabilities*, 53(5), pp. 354–365. doi: 10.1177/0022219420920377. Epub 2020 May 26. PMID: 32452713; PMCID: PMC8183124.

Walker, N. (2014). Neurodiversity: Terms and definitions. Neuroqueer, 27 September. [Online] Available at: https://neuroqueer.com/neurodiversity-terms-and-definitions/

Walker, N. (2021). *Neuroqueer Heresies: Notes on the Neurodiversity Paradigm, Autistic Empowerment, and Postnormal Possibilities.* Autonomous Press.

Warrier, V., Greenberg, D. M., Weir, E., Buckingham, C., Smith, P., Lai, M. C., Allison, C. and Baron-Cohen, S. (2020). Elevated rates of autism, other neurodevelopmental and psychiatric diagnoses, and autistic traits in transgender and gender-diverse individuals. *Nature Communications*, 11(1), 3959. https://doi.org/10.1038/s41467-020-17794-1. PMID: 32770077; PMCID: PMC7415151.

Wissell S, Karimi L, Serry T, Furlong L, Hudson J. "You Don't Look Dyslexic": Using the Job Demands-Resource Model of Burnout to Explore Employment Experiences of Australian Adults with Dyslexia. Int J Environ Res Public Health. 2022 Aug 28;19(17):10719. doi: 10.3390/ijerph191710719. PMID: 36078435; PMCID: PMC9518213.

Wood, T. (2022). IKEA products are named the way they are because founder was dyslexic. [Online] LADbible. Available at: www.ladbible.com/news/ikea-product-naming-system-20221025 [Accessed 28 July 2024].

World Economic Forum. (2022). Explainer: Neurodivergence and mental health. [Online] World Economic Forum. Available at: www.weforum.org/agenda/2022/10/explainer-neurodivergence-mental-health/ [Accessed 3 August 2024].

World Health Organization. (2022). Covid-19 pandemic triggers 25% increase in prevalence of anxiety and depression worldwide. [Online] World Health Organization. Available at: www.who.int/news/item/02-03-2022-covid-19-pandemic-triggers-25-increase-in-prevalence-of-anxiety-and-depression-worldwide [Accessed 3 August 2024].

World Health Organization. (2023). Autism spectrum disorders. [Online] World Health Organization. Available at: www.who.int/news-room/fact-sheets/detail/autism-spectrum-disorders

Young, E. (2022). Some people are "disabled". Others "live with" or "have a disability". Here's the difference between identity-first and person-first language. [Online] ABC News. Available at: www.abc.net.au/news/2022-12-01/disability-language-identity-person-first/101597752

Zajic, M. C. and Gudknecht, J. (2024). Person- and Identity-first Language in Autism Research: A Systematic Analysis of Abstracts from 11 Autism Journals. *Autism: The International Journal of Research and Practice.* https://doi.org/10.1177/1362361324 1241202.

Zhu, B., 2023. What steps can be taken to reduce unconscious bias in the workplace? *Academic Journal of Management and Social Sciences*, 5(1), pp.34–50. ISSN 2958-4396.

Zhu, F., Liu, B., Kuang, D., Zhu, X., Bi, X., Song, Y., Quan, T. and Yang, Y. (2023). The Association between Physical Activity and Sleep in Adult ADHD Patients with Stimulant Medication Use. *Frontiers in Psychiatry*, 14, 1236636. https://doi.org/10.3389/fpsyt.2023.1236 636. PMID: 38076701; PMCID: PMC10698374.

Zindell, J. L. (2024). Neurodiversity in Workplace. [Online] M.S. in Leadership, 128. Available at: https://scholars.unh.edu/ms_leadership/128

Index